Rediscovering
Herbert Horne

Rediscovering Herbert Horne

Poet

Architect

Typographer

Art Historian

Ian Fletcher

Contents

ELT PRESS
Department of English
University of North Carolina
Greensboro, NC 27412-5001

Number Three

in the

1880-1920 British Authors Series

Distributed in Europe by

Colin Smythe, Ltd.
Gerrards Cross, Buckinghamshire
England SL9 8XA

Copyright ELT Press © 1990

All Rights Reserved

ISBN 0-944318-02-9

Acid-Free paper ∞

Library of Congress Cataloging in Publication Data

90-081094

Loraine

Agnes

Genevra

Illustrations

Chapter number/ Illustration number

There was a young fellow of Chelsea
Who said "I've old masters to sell, see!"
When they said "They're a fraud"
He replied "No. They're Claude
And you critics may go sirs to Hell, see!"

Selwyn Image

Foreword

Ian Fletcher has written so well about the world of the 1890s that it is hard to believe that his extraordinary creativity has ceased. Now thanks to the dedication of Robert Langenfeld, Loraine Fletcher, and Kathleen Mason Driskell the book that he was working on for many years, in the midst of doing so much else, has been made ready for the press. Perhaps the most important piece published previously on Horne was Ian Fletcher's own, written as long ago as 1970: "Herbert Horne: The Earlier Phase," in the *English Miscellany*, edited by Mario Praz who rivalled both Horne and Fletcher in the amazing and fertile range of his interests. Ian Fletcher had the rare ability to explore thoroughly and perceptively the many different worlds necessary to know for a discussion of the life and accomplishments of Herbert Horne.

Some years ago, writing about the acquisition by the Stanford University Library of a small but significant collection of Horne material, I attempted, as an introduction to the collection, to provide an overview of Horne's life. What Ian Fletcher has written is full of rich particularity and insight. But I thought it might be helpful to the reader, drawing on my earlier piece, to recount very briefly Horne's career to serve as a preface to a more detailed depiction and analysis of his accomplishments.

Herbert Horne was a man of wide-ranging talents. He began his professional career as an architect, but quickly branched out into other creative activities. He became a fine designer of books and type, an editor, a poet, an expert

ix

collector of art, and a widely recognized art historian and critic.

Horne was in the tradition of William Morris, although more consciously an aesthete and lacking Morris's intense concern for politics. As the century turned, Horne made his mark in advanced artistic circles. His varied career tells us a good deal about what was happening then in the world of design, literature, art criticism, and architecture.

He began training with a surveyor, but he saw some drawings by the designer and architect A. H. Mackmurdo, who was in the process of starting his own building and design practice, and persuaded his father that he should be allowed to apprentice himself to him. Mackmurdo was one of the most interesting English figures in the generation after William Morris—working in his wake, influenced by him, yet disagreeing with some of his ideas. Mackmurdo was also a disciple and friend of John Ruskin's. As one of a growing group who believed that an architect should involve himself in all aspects of a building, Mackmurdo in the early 1880s designed in an exhilarating and exciting way.

At about this time, Mackmurdo, Horne, and the designer Selwyn Image brought into being a loose association of craftsmen in various mediums known as the Century Guild. The Century Guild was a design group that was anxious to strike out in a new direction; it was at odds with Victorian styles and heralded what was to come in the twentieth century. It was into this hothouse of new design that Horne plunged at the tender age of eighteen, and he was so successful that two years later he became Mackmurdo's architectural partner.

Mackmurdo and Horne actually designed only a few buildings, in Knightsbridge and elsewhere, but they were all striking, fresh, imaginative, comparatively simple, and representative of a new style that did not simply ransack the past. The partners also designed numerous objects and materials to be used in their "new" architecture—delightful furniture, textiles, wallpapers. They obviously felt that they could do whatever they set their minds to.

Horne also participated in the literary life of London. Mackmurdo's office was at 20 Fitzroy Street, and the house became practically a literary and musical commune. Members of the Rhymers' Club met there and Arnold Dolmetsch, who recreated ancient instruments and played older music as it was performed in its own time, gave concerts. (One of the harpsichords Dolmetsch built was decorated by Horne together with Image and Helen Coombe, who would later marry the Bloomsbury painter and art critic Roger Fry.)

In addition, Horne was active in the related world of books, book design, and the founding of an important art magazine, the *Century Guild Hobby Horse*. The first issue of the magazine appeared in 1884; then between 1886 and 1892 twenty-eight issues were published; the final three appeared in a different format in 1893-94. As art historian Gillian Naylor has observed, "the *Hobby Horse* was the first of the art-oriented literary magazines of the 1880s and 1890s." The magazine was as committed as the Century Guild itself to total design, to the belief that every component of the printed page—type, margins, illustrations—was in a vital relationship to every other and that the journal itself must be a work of art. In keeping with this belief, it was printed entirely on hand-made paper.

Although it had few subscribers, the *Hobby Horse* was very influential. It helped inspire Morris with the possibilities of good design. In 1888 Bernard Berenson—later to be less admiring and rather a rival of Horne's—met Horne and saw him as *the* successor to William Morris and "the great man of the next generation, as architect, painter, poet, fine critic, and editor of the *Hobby Horse*."

Horne also did some editing, presumably to supplement his income which was probably limited at the time. He was a good friend of Ernest Rhys, who later became editor of Every-man Library. Rhys wrote the introduction for Horne's edition of Robert Herrick's *Hesperides*, published in 1887, the first work by Horne to appear in book form. The next year, along with Havelock Ellis, Arthur Symons, and A. Wilson Verity, Horne edited, in the Mermaid Series, a group of seventeenth-century plays.

For a few more years Horne continued his activities in London. But he and Mackmurdo were on increasingly bad terms and in 1890 the architectural partnership dissolved. He had an enjoyable life in London—he was a devotee of ballet girls, as were Selwyn Image and Reverend Steward Headlam, the Christian Socialist priest who formed a guild for stage "artistes." All three enjoyed going to the Empire Theatre, and they supported Winston Churchill when he fought against the attempt to shut down its promenade, which was frequented by ladies of dubious virtue.

Horne became very fond of Florence and spent more and more time in the city. Finally he settled there permanently in 1900, perhaps to make money as an art dealer. He was a con-noisseur and an art collector, and in Italy that aspect of his life would take in even greater importance. Even before he left London, he had amassed a considerable collection of English drawings; once he had settled in Florence, however, most of these were sold.

In Florence, Horne continued his dedication to the life of art, but primarily as an art historian and art expert. For a while he was quite friendly with Bernard Berenson, dedicating a translation of Vasari's essay on Leonardo Da Vinci (1903) to him. Horne wrote less material specifically about art history than Berenson, but he did publish one masterpiece in 1908, his mammoth study of Botticelli. Botticelli, although cham-pioned by Ruskin and Pater, had not yet acquired his present canonical status, and Horne's work was crucial in that progres-sion. The study has recently been reissued by the Princeton

University Press with a foreword by John Pope-Hennessy, who states that it is "the best monograph in English on an Italian painter. . . . As an interpretation of Botticelli and his work it has never been surpassed." The art historian Fritz Saxl remarked about Horne that he was "perhaps the most accomplished art historian of art whom [England] has ever produced."

Horne's last triumph of aestheticism was the acquisition in 1911 of a handsome Florentine palazzo, now known as the Museo Horne, which in a gesture of thanks toward his adopted city, he bequeathed to Florence after his death there in 1916. Ian Fletcher has presented us with a rich picture of Horne, in all the multiplicity of his talents and accomplishments. The book that follows celebrates both men.

Peter Stansky
Stanford University

Preface

Before 1900, Herbert Horne's life is a field more appropriate to the literary historian. A historian of art is a requisite for some just estimate of Horne's activities after that date. To the latter term, I cannot pretend, so I touch tentatively, if extensively, on Horne as collector and as art historian. Nonetheless it seems proper enough to attempt a gathering—as Horne himself might have phrased it—of "all that we know" about a figure who was in some ways so highly typical of, though in others so severely antithetical to, that mysterious precipitation, the 1890s.

Horne was a person of acute virtuosity, embodying in himself some reflex of that Renaissance breadth and *finesse* he so admired: poet, craftsman, book designer, typographer, connoisseur, architect, art historian. In a period known for the the brevity of its lives, the narrowness of its range, its perpetual flight to the peripheral, Horne's sanity, practicality, sobriety and variousness are particularly remarkable. Yet he exposed himself to the representative movements, temperaments and forms of the end of the century—to arts and crafts, the aesthetic movement, the Church and Stage Guild, the higher journalism, the Rhymers' Club, Pater, Mackmurdo, Morris, Selwyn Image, Stewart Headlam, Johnson, Dowson, Dolmetsch, Fry, Berenson, Wilde, Ross, Beerbohm, Symons. Still he remained, or rather he became, his own man: equably so, whether in Chelsea, Bloomsbury, or Florence. Frugal, contained, learned, Horne impressed observers with a stylized opacity which attracted curiosity and sometimes resentment.

Where possible I have culled unpublished sources and should like to acknowledge the generosity of those who have permitted their use. This is the moment and the place to record my thanks in particular to Lisa Tickner, Linda Dowling, Dr. Peter Stansky, and Mrs. T. C. Dugdale for help and encouragement. Signor Tito Messeri, son of Horne's housekeeper, gave me free access to Horne's house in Florence.

I must concede that this little book is but a beginning, a rediscovery, we might say, of this alarmingly versatile man's contributions to the art and culture of his time. Though my tenuous health has made the final stages of writing demanding, I nevertheless am sanguine that my purpose here is valuable: to sketch Horne's varied achievements and thus offer a groundwork for other scholars to build upon. What is needed of course is not only an edited collection of Horne's essays and closer analysis of his diverse work, but a full-scale biography. Those considerable tasks I must leave to others.

CHAPTER 1

The Early Phase

Herbert Horne's name is probably more familiar to historians of art than to those concerned with literary history.[1] His work on Botticelli remains authoritative and he preserves a minor but honourable place in the history of design, largely through his connexion with A. H. Mackmurdo and the Century Guild. But Horne's activities were not confined to these fields. He was a scholarly and elegant typographer and book designer, a connoisseur who on small means built up a remarkable collection of eighteenth-century water colours, and as an architect he made a small but distinct contribution.

From 1886 to 1891 he was virtual editor of the *Century Guild Hobby Horse* and he edited its successor the *Hobby Horse* which ran from 1893 to 1894. This was perhaps the most complete example of an English "Total Art" periodical with its hand-made paper, specially designed initials, borders and typography, and programmatic content. That content places it in the late Pre-Raphaelite Arts and Crafts tradition, but with occasional anticipations of Art Nouveau. Horne was also one of the minor poets of the period, and although he was only twenty-six when the Rhymers' Club was formed, his authority in matters of taste was already such that he was able to assume the role of mentor. With Lionel Johnson, W. B. Yeats and, to a lesser degree, Arthur Symons, he gave that *cénacle* such coherence of doctrine as it possessed. Yet in spite of his distinguished gifts and achievements, Horne had no place in the *Dictionary of National Biography*, though he himself contributed to the earlier, more useful volumes. His poetry was only part of his many-sided activities, and was abandoned early for severer pursuits.

Herbert Percy Horne was born in London on 18 February 1864 at the house of his maternal grandfather John Rowland Gibson, a surgeon, of 10 Russell Square, London. He was the son of Horace Horne and Hannah Louisa Porter.[2] Horne's father's fortune has been derived from and had declined with the business of horse carriers.[3] From his father, Horne derived his ardent interest in collecting. By the time Herbert was attending Miss Moore's day school at 8 Hereford Street, Kensington, at about the age of ten, he had already begun to collect scraps of old glass and to take brass rubbings. Here he came under the influence of one of his masters, Daniel Barron Brightwell, art critic and later editor of the *Birmingham Weekly Post*, whose work appeared under the pseudonym "Rufus." Horne was to remember Brightwell always with respect and affection, though his tastes naturally diverged from those of his old master. At Miss Moore's he also encountered Randall Davies who was to be his friend for over forty years. Davies was deeply interested in literature, art history and collecting, and was to become Horne's literary executor.

After a period at Kensington Grammar School, Horne was articled to a relative, George Vigers, who practiced as a surveyor in Old Jewry in the City of London. About 1880, the Horne family had moved to 6 Newton Grove in the West London garden suburb of Bedford Park, built by E. W. Godwin, Norman Shaw, E. J. May and others in a style which G. K. Chesterton was to describe as "sometimes Elizabethan and sometimes Queen Anne, apparently under the impression that the two sovereigns were identical." During his adolescent years, therefore, Horne moved in what can fairly be described as an artistic *ambient*, for Bedford Park, if not quite the aesthetic quarter of popular journalistic description, had many notable residents, literary men, actors, academics, and was full of talking clubs and amateur theatricals.[4] Probably at this time Horne read Pater's *Renaissance* and acquired his first interest in the quattrocento.

Towards the end of 1880, Horne had encountered some of A. H. Mackmurdo's drawings, obtained an introduction and enquired whether Mackmurdo would be prepared to give instruction in architectural drawing and design. Horne probably joined Mackmurdo about 1882, the year in which Mackmurdo had founded the Century Guild. This was the first of the Arts and Crafts Guilds specifically designed to unite the arts. Impressed by Horne's abilities, Mackmurdo decided to take him into partnership, and a letter from Horace Horne to Mackmurdo of 2 June 1883 sets out the terms of agreement: for the first year Herbert Horne was to receive fifty pounds and commission on work bought by him; at the end of that year he was to be taken into full partnership, receiving for the next three years a third and subsequently one half of the profits.[5]

On both Mackmurdo and his close friend, Selwyn Image, Horne seems to have made a bold impression, and the Century Guild offices on the first floor at 28 Southampton Street were filled with discussion, verse-writing and theorizing in general about art and life. The archives of the Museo Horne, Florence, contain a number of manuscripts which record Horne's views: a rather sentimental Anglo-Catholicism and Pre-Raphaelitism counterpoint to the harsher antinomian precepts of Blake. Horne struggled toward the recognition of the dual elements in his nature—the voluptuary and the precisian—which as Fritz Saxl pointed out were to be finally and fruitfully united in the passionately accurate scholarship of his last years. The following rough extract, for example, seems to cut Blake down to the size of Selwyn Image, for its doctrine anticipates Image's polemics against Impressionist art:

> Male and female created he them—the dual, the knower
> and the lover
> the poetic nature is the marriage of Heaven & Hell—
> You shall be as Gods knowing good and evil—
> The torrid and the frigid interwove—entangled
> recreated each of each all these finer battles which
> escape a coarse crude net of words.
> On his right is science—pure, cold, intellect and the
> religion of such intellect—puritanism, that would be
> destroyer of art. On his left pure naked flesh where
> religion is lust ever striving to seduce art.
> Body and soul one in the scientist's sense of the
> word—one in the monk's sense of the word.
> Therefore the influence of the body must survive with the influence
> of the soul—both are eternal.
> Neither the immortality of the Atheists; nor the
> immortality of the theologians.
> The power of great creation, not of great invention—
> Inspiration not memory—idealism not realism.[6]

Other aphorisms are close to Stewart Headlam's and Image's sacramental and anti-ascetic ideals.

Further discussions with Image centered on the relations between the arts. We find Horne experimenting with a "lyrical novel" under the influence of De Quincey's *Suspiria de Profundis*. Early in 1883 he outlined a theory of poetry combining arguments which resemble Poe's exaltation of lyric verse with a positivist theory of progress that reflects Mackmurdo's influence. Music is hinted at as a type of the arts, but his doctrine is again crossed by Anglo-Catholic and Blakeian influences: lyric, which to Horne seems peculiarly appropriate to the present age, is defined as the "arbitrary use of the concrete in order to idealise human feeling." This leads to a condemnation of Tennyson's *Idylls*. The message is "that everywhere the flesh is hindering and confining the work of the spirit. Surely all know, or should know, by this time that the flesh is the spirit and the spirit is the flesh—that if the spirit is good the flesh is good & vice-versa. The Idylls of the King are but a blaize [*sic*] of fine words flung up on a theological foundation that virtually was rotten three centuries ago." Mackmurdo's influence emerges in the attempt to determine a historical rhythm in the development of poetry, a development from Epic (action) to Lyric (feeling):

> The evolution of our ideas has always ascended from the more special to the more general: & therefore from Action thro thought and feeling & not from feeling to action. . . . By the law of the development of the more special before the more general, we should expect to find the Epic spirit completed before the Lyric: as we do. Poetry from being special at first will at last attain a vast generalization.

The propositional form of the argument is Positivist, but the doctrine's interest largely relates to the fragments of a programme in the circle of the Rhymers' Club as these are recalled by Yeats in his *Autobiographies*. Much of the 1890s poetic theory is latent in these remarks: the rejection of action and discursiveness, the reaction from Tennyson because of his "impurities," the exaltation of the lyrical and the subjective. However, Horne rather inconsistently attempted to justify his notions on optimistic and Positivist grounds, which ran counter to all that we know of the Rhymers' beliefs.

Close to the theories of the Rhymers' and Selwyn Image is another note written at the beginning of 1884, in which Ruskin's view of Nature is rejected virtually in terms of Blake's Trees of Life and Science. Imagination leads to a complete historical relativism:

> All things exist only as we are in possession of their mental equivalents. It would be as true to say that Shakespeare existed at the time of Aristotle as the then unknown planets. All things were from the first; but to us now, only those things of which we are mentally in possession.
>
> The tree of Giotto, the tree of the Purist, the tree of the Ruskinian were realities to their several producers—realities to the last sense of the word.
>
> Again it would be said that the Ruskinian tree approaching almost with identity to the photograph must be true absolutely in the same proportion. Who will not admit a photograph of a face to be wanting altogether in certain qualities! A photograph of a tree is then also wanting in these qualities.

In other extracts, Horne has clearly attended to Mackmurdo's historical method in *Wren's City Churches* (1882). There Mackmurdo altogether excluded the archaeological and comparative emphasis on mere architectural vocabulary, fashionable at the time, concentrating on close analysis of buildings in isolation, together with a summary reference to the contexts of Wren's work—social, political, artistic, literary. This was an alternative also to Pater's intuitive approach and helped to deflect Horne's interest from the Medieval period to the Renaissance. Another set of notes in the Museo Horne, probably dating from 1884, reveals that the seventeenth century had become Horne's ideal moment in English culture, challenging the present:

> An age of no beliefs & so of no architecture: an age that must purify: an age that has found the desire of life in science, the knowledge of appearances. An age that has built itself a city greater than the cities of wrath, a city of iron and matchboarding . . . which is to say of rust and of tinder.

In the seventeenth century, gardening, architecture and literature had been properly associated; the architectural sense, indeed, had been fruitfully diffused over every art:

Reasons for beginning with the Renaissance. During the early Renaissance every "artist" has the architectural sense, the cut of the two
people kneeling before a seated figure & other figures standing at
back—towards end of book. True of Giotto's art. The round temple in
Raphael's cartoons. Contrast this with modern paintings & the architecture in them. The whole Elizabethan period wanting in this
architectural feeling, both in literature and in architecture.

And recurring to his own ambition in poetry to reconcile the
"torrid and the frigid":

Not only of poetry but of every art:—
In expression restrained, but in the matter
expressed free and licensed.
Milton's Samson.
Bach's Fugues.
Ghirlandajo's portrait. Nat. Gal. staircase.
Chosen because the architectural effect is
obtained by coral necklace, scroll, & book . . .
and very slightly by purely architectural lines.

Such enthusiasms and detractions led Horne "to trace the
Muses upward to their spring," and in the English tradition that
involved a shift of emphasis from Wren to Inigo Jones. He was
to contribute a poem on Jones to the *Century Guild Hobby
Horse* for January 1886 and to furnish an article, full of too
generous attributions, on the admired architect for the *Dictionary of National Biography*. But Jones himself led Horne to
Palladio, Italy, and ultimately to Vitruvius. Horne was to visit
Italy for the first time in 1889 and from the middle of the 1890s
to spend much of his time there.

As we shall see, the importance of these extracts is that
they reveal Horne in this early phase gradually freeing himself
from the influence of Image and Mackmurdo, the pupil eventually becoming the master.

CHAPTER **2**

Horne and Some Contemporaries

Frailty of body and strength of personality is the impression Horne made on many of his contemporaries. Yet such strength of personality was only evident on long acquaintance. Horne was never a ready talker and the very judiciousness of his talk tended to leave a false effect of dilettantism. Like Pater, he seems to have been a man of low vitality, though he was no celibate. Besides frail health (Horne and his sister both died in their early fifties), the family had inherited mental instability.[1]

In the literary memoirs of the 1890s, Horne is prominent. On Henry Sirr, a prosaic associate of Mackmurdo's, he made an unfavourable impression: "I met Herbert Horne once and thought he looked as if some fresh air would do him good."[2] The double-headed nightingale, "Michael Field," describes him as having "squeezed features, eyes that are drawn like a single thickened line repeated, spent complexion and a grin. . . . He is not a milk-sop, but a tea-sop—mild, effeminate, with an art aroma, a choiceness." The ladies, however, were more charitable: "There is defect in every inch of Horne's face, and yet what pleasant defect—it is used by sensitiveness so well that it

becomes interesting and has a kindly appeal," though he is
also found to be "sick and clayey."[3]

This art aroma and choice mildness equally offended
John Davidson, whom Yeats records in *Autobiographies* as
bursting out with "if a man must be a connoisseur, let him be a
connoisseur of women." Yet that precisely Horne seems to
have been. Indeed, he went one better: he was a connoisseur
of both men and women.

William Rothenstein, with a painter's eye, remarked
Horne's pale face, the hard red lips, and other observers
sensed some contrast or tension between pallid cheeks and
startlingly vivid mouth. Edgar Jepson found him "dark and
Italianate with regular features and pale, with curiously red
lips. . . . I have never known a man colder and more reserved
and self-centred, a purist of purists," yet "in spite of his cold-
ness Horne must on occasion have burned with considerable
ardour, for he loved always the prettiest of the ladies who
adorned the circle."[4]

It is not easy to comment on Horne's emotional life. The
tone of his letters to Jepson in the later 1890s is scabrous, that
of the disappointed ageing bachelor. But it is certain that he
began to haunt the music-halls in his late teens and this led to
adventures. In 1883 he seems to have been in love with one of
the actresses at the Gaiety, perhaps Nellie Farren, and if so it is
hardly surprising that the affair remained on a strictly platonic
footing. Both Horne and Image were friendly with one of the
unknown's friends, Ada Smith, with her "wonderful gold hair,"
and Image made a small drawing in red chalk of Ada, which he
presented to Horne.

Among the Symons papers at Princeton, however, there is
an account of Horne based partly on Symons's own memoirs
and partly on a conversation he had recently had with Selwyn
Image on 3 June 1924.[5] This all seems rather coloured by the
sick mentality of Symons's later years, but contains some acute

comments nonetheless. According to Symons, Horne was over-sexed and indifferently heterosexual and homosexual, while his father was a shady character who had a disastrous effect on his children. Symons quotes the following observation from Image:

> His insanity showed itself in a most vexatious manner when, annoyed and made furious by some commission he had wanted to have and which was given to me, we had a fierce quarrel. He disappeared for two years, no one knew whither. It appeared that he had gone so as to escape from charges of the worst kind against him to some part of Italy. He never wrote me one letter, in fact I heard nothing about him until he came back. Then we returned to our former friendly relations. . . . A feminine trait in Horne was his adoration of flattery. Whenever he was flattered he literally expanded. . . . There is one point I must emphasise: that Horne was the most secretive man I have ever known, absolutely and always. And this was one of the worst qualities in his sinister nature. He avoided more than anyone I have ever known the least reference to what he did with his nights, let alone what he did with his days. I had no inkling of Horne's homosexuality. You are probably right in what you have said. So abnormal, so self-centred a man with a taint of insanity in his veins, is as often as not [not] responsive of the actions he commits. That is of course only a side issue to this sinister question.

Symons then relates his first meeting with Horne:

> It was my evil genius, like Casanova's, who deluded me into entering the same house where Image lived, where I encountered Herbert Horne, whose shifting and treacherous eyes were one of the certain signs of what was inimical in the man. He was short,[6] dark, neat, very worldly looking. His manner was cold and restrained, with a mingling of insolence and diffidence. He never mentioned the word "love" except to jest at it; and yet there could be no doubt as to his meaning. His whole attitude was one of patient waiting. Such women were set apart in his carefully arranged life from matters which absorbed him in other senses. He was one of those critics who would do any man's work but their own. When he sat down to write something dry and hard came into the words. He always chafed a little under what seemed an unnecessary devotion. On principle, he did not like clever

women. He had his own very deliberate theory of values, and one value was never allowed to interfere with another. A devoted, discreet, amateur of women, he appreciated women really for their own sex.

For several years we were on rather friendly terms. I rarely called on him in his rooms in Kings' Bench Walk, not far from where George Moore lived. He had a terrible habit of calling on me in Fountain Court when I least wanted to see him. We were most friendly when he was keeping Muriel Broadbent. It was with a Latin solemnity Selwyn Image and myself signed a legal document—for the rent of the place in which she stayed—that she was an honest woman. She was frightfully nice and kind to me; one of those women who are sensual and excitable though not passionate. There was something bright and attractive about her, apart from her erotic nature. . . . She often took refuge with me when her men made her exasperated; and when I opened the door after she had knocked on it, she burst in, flushed and feverish, then flung herself on the sofa and became hysterical. She got mixed up in an indiscriminate fashion with young lords and with younger poets, with Jews and with Gentiles, with painters and prose writers; and to such an extent that they all got mixed up and jumbled together in that queer head of hers. When finally she had to marry a man of good position,[7] there were terrible scenes between her and her keeper. Once I was walking with him in Chelsea when Muriel waved her hand to us from a cab; his face became livid and furious; and in his surly voice he said "Let us turn down the next street and escape her."

Horne exacted more from the women he was mixed up with than any man had a natural right to exact. Outwardly, he was the animal on the prey; but in his complex character, inwardly, one divined his abnormal passion for men: he was at once a hard liver, a Sadist and Pervert.

Horne was fiendishly jealous, cold, cruel, calculating; always aware of the insidious ambushes into which he might fall, which he took an immense trouble in avoiding. Sexually endowed to an excess which was morbid, an abominable sense of his fascination when he was least so came over him. Intensely avid in following up sinister adventures by which he hoped to profit, he let me in to some of his cunning plots which so often to his disgust were abject failures. He was unpassionate; he never had any passionate adventures; whatever passion he had went in the wrong direction; he was literally incapable of inspiring either love or passion in women's hearts; and if by chance he wakened a spark of it in any of them, that was soon extinguished. He raised in many of these women such an aversion that he became to them literally insupportable. This was his lifelong grievance.

Such a man as Horne who never marries, never could have, and who lives, as one phrases it, alone for the greater part of his life must have resources of his own, not an inner contentment, from which he imbibes as from drugs and drinks ineffable sensation. . . . In lives such as these, there is a kind of aching *Sterility*, which may or may not make them barren of success. Then the nausea of a series of disgusts, the odor of corruption; satiety, disillusion; and in these cases the absolute need of a prodigious mental activity, an aloofness from the atmosphere of the common world; in which these create an atmosphere of their own, which might be peopled with mocking and contemptuous shadows and phantom shapes. I am inclined to end this study in morbidity with a quotation from Pater, in his somewhat cynical review of *The Picture of Dorian Gray* by Oscar Wilde. "But his story is also a vivid, though carefully considered, exposure of the corruption of a soul, with a very plain moral pushed home, to the effect that vice and crime make people coarse and ugly."

Symons had been in communication with Horne as early as 1887 and they soon became fairly closely acquainted. They toured Belgium together and in 1895 Symons passed a number of months in Italy with Horne. Both had a passion for the music hall; both were *littérateurs*; both had a determined interest in women, particularly ballet dancers and ladies of the night; but Horne's was the more casual and successful. The letters between the two take us to 1895 when there seems to have been a break, probably brought about by Horne and accentuated by the increasing amount of time now spent by him in Florence.

The Symons of the 1890s was naïve, energetic, not to say pushing—an egoist somewhat devoid of an ego. His letters betray the man; though they fail in mastering the witty dandiacal obliquities of malice so dear to the *fin de siècle*, they are briskly empty without acuity of phrase, catching at surfaces. Yeats praises Symons's femininity of personality, a sympathetic mirror that reflected and crystallized the ideas of others, but the defect of these qualities can be gathered from his correspondence.

In that memorable summer of 1895 when, with Conder and Beardsley, the *Savoy* was planned, Symons tried hard to persuade Horne to come to Dieppe. But the invitation was ignored. Symons had little to offer him either personally or intellectually. Horne was moving away from "appreciative" criticism. His new friends were connoisseurs, dealers, art historians, art critics: men such as Roger Fry, Robert Ross, Charles Loeser and Bernard Berenson. Symons, with his provincial conscience, the endless parade of his versified sins humourlessly magnified and multiplied beyond all necessity, became a figure of fun, as Horne's letters to Edgar Jepson testify. Those furnish a sharper, less obsessive counterpart to Symons's image of Horne. By February 1896 Horne had come to see that *fin de siècle* London was finished. If for Beerbohm the Rhymers' favoured pub, the Crown, had always been dull (full of nameless minor poets, cocottes and unfrocked clergymen), for Horne it had fallen into "a slough of dullness."

That the poet Symons should "waste his sweetness upon the desert air of some unfrequented pub goes to my heart. . . . And that the shadow of respectability should stand in the way of Smithers" he naturally lamented. From another letter it appears that

> Symons is expected to arrive in Rome as soon as he is quit of his engagements with Smithers. He is invited there . . . by an Italian Count who holds some office about the Papal Court . . . What is not yet generally known is that he is expected to be received into the Church upon his arrival there; and so presently join one of the religious orders, that in the sickroom of the monastic life, he may devote the rest of his days in expiation of the horrid vices and enormities of his past life.[8]

And on 10 October 1898 Horne asks Jepson if he has read "the newest 'little Arthur' newly arrived from Spain, and reeking in the 'Saturday' [Review] with the blood of bull-fights." So much for Symons's impressionist travel pieces.

The most insistent topic, though, was the distance between Symons's erotic ambitions and his bodily accoutrement. In a letter of 26 February 1897, Horne congratulates Jepson on some delicately obscene verses satirising Symons and suggests that the climax of his correspondent's career as a lubricous poet will consist in composing

> a whole Priapeia on the subject of our little Arthur's tool. When little Arthur's epic appears, you will, I trust, show how far in the arts of the smelling sentimental, the singer of drawers surpasses the singer of petticoats—joking apart, your discourse on the hearth-rug bard was severely admirable.

An earlier letter juxtaposes Horne's present interests with Symons as representative of a tepid past:

> As I have abandoned all other pursuits, except that of mounting my drawings in bistre and gold, an equable occupation which I only occasionally break by writing in the *Saturday Review*, I have been unable to write to you from the want of those experiences which alone could enable me to surpass your own wit in your own way. However, I chanced to wander this evening down that rural lane, Piccadilly, looking like the darned Gerard of old, for wayside flowers; when I chanced upon a very irregular specimen. I had met with it before—years ago in my wanderings; and the conversation which passed between is not so unpleasing, that I should not send you a notable passage or so.

The Flower:	'Ow's your friend?
Myself:	What friend?
The Flower:	You know—'im as lent me a book.
Myself:	What do you mean?
The Flower:	What lives in the Temple—by that fountain sort of place.

Myself:	Oh! I know. Don't know. Haven't seen him lately
	(pause). What the devil are you grinning like that for?
The Flower:	Oh, 'e never come home wif me!
Myself:	Didn't he!
The Flower:	But he tried to 'ave Minnie tho'.
Myself:	Did he!
The Flower:	Little winkle of a thing! He couldn't do nuffing wif it!

Now, my dear Jepson, supply the plot or the incident, or what not; and add the necessary inflection: and a short story is made to your hand, which should not be unworthy of the higher magazines, such as the Yellow Book, or—the Savoy.

Neither the *Yellow Book* nor Symons's *Savoy* much appealed to Horne. Finding (and filching) a copy of the *Savoy* at Fiesole he wrote to Jepson on 9 March 1896: "Symons at Dieppe might honestly be taken for one of Harrod's young men . . . out for his summer trip. For silliness and middle-class bad taste it would be impossible to surpass it. As a piece of writing it is certainly very clever." Nor was Beardsley's *Under the Hill* approved:

For an honest *lusus ineptus* written with knowledge and zest I have nothing but admiration; if kept like all the higher aspirations of the human mind, it should be within the proper privacy of the closet. But the concluding sentence of Beardsley's novel appears to me worthy only of a schoolboy: the [illegible] in the asparagus and the satyrs could occur only to a 6th form boy who is still virginal of the other sex. But you see what a Philistine I have become.

Horne's displeasure may well have been accentuated by his recognition that two brief stories which Symons contributed to the *Savoy*, "The Childhood of Lucy Newcome" and "Pages from the Life of Lucy Newcome," were *écrites à clef* founded on the biography of Muriel Broadbent. This second story has as its climax the moment Lucy begins her career of gallantry as a consequence of being abandoned by a lover and left with a baby which she has to support by drudging in a laundry. The baby dies and Lucy decides that she might as well become the mistress of an elderly man who has already begun delicate advances. Manuscripts in the Princeton Collection and at Arizona State University make it clear that Symons intended a novel à la Goncourt, based not on continuous narrative but on recording significant sensations. Some parts of this novel were written and in it both Symons and Horne appear, though the presentation of both is curiously colourless.[9]

But Horne makes a far from colourless appearance in Beardsley's romance. Besides its pornographic travesty, involving self-parody and at a deeper level the irreducible dilemmas of the *avant garde* of the Nineties, *Under the Hill* (and more elaborately its fuller version *The Story of Venus and Tannhäuser*) involves much recognisable local satire. The contained tensions of Horne's character are presented through the wild incompatibilities of that learned libertine and corrupter of innocence, Sporion: "a tall, slim, depraved young man with a slight stoop, a troubled walk, an oval impassible face with its olive skin drawn lightly over the bone, strong, scarlet lips, long Japanese eyes, and a great gilt toupee."[10] The physical reminiscence, minus the toupee of course, is clear. Pursuing his "Bacchanals," Sporion with his brilliant followers enter an Arcadian valley peopled by innocent nymphs and shepherds "hoping to experience a new *frisson* in the destruction of some shepherd's or some satyr's *naïveté*, and the infusion of their venom among the dwellers of the woods." Sporion abundantly succeeds in his intention and so represents the peculiarly Decadent fascination with barbarism: those underlying affinities between beau and brute, Pastoralism and the dance, Herrick and, as we shall see, the dancers of the Alhambra and the Empire music halls. Beardsley know-

ingly associates Horne and Sporion; the names are obviously
connected homophonically and historically.

Ernest Dowson too expresses his own sense of the incon-
gruities of Horne's character, admirer of ancient music and
haunter of the stage door at midnight. Meeting Horne and
Image together in this role, Dowson observed: "There was
something eminently grotesque in the juxtaposition. Horne
very erect & slim & aesthetic—& Image the most dignified man
in London, a sort of cross in appearance between a secular
abbe & Baudelaire, with a manner du 18me siecle—waiting in
a back passage to be escort to ballet girls whom they don't
even —— !!!" Dowson may possibly have been wrong about
that.

CHAPTER 3

The Poet and His Poetry

By the middle 1880s Horne had become a habitué of the Alhambra. For a short while it was a circus, but developed in the late 1870s and 1880s into one of the centres of London nightlife. The entertainment, as at the Empire, which opened in 1887, consisted of ballet, singing and variety turns, and the 1890s were to be the golden age of this type of entertainment, murdered by D.O.R.A. and embalmed by T. S. Eliot. The Alhambra and Empire were regarded as theatres rather than music halls. They hardly provided family entertainment. The principal feature at the Alhambra was a salon where the ladies of chorus and ballet mingled with the audience, and not unnaturally, as a contemporary chronicler put it, "some of the fair members of the company were eventually translated to the upper house." At the Empire, the main attraction was the promenade, which resembled an indoor Piccadily: a stalking-ground for middle-range prostitutes. In such a context, Headlam, Image and Horne would meet their women friends and adjourn to the Crown in Charing Cross Road.[1]

As has been frequently noted, the theatre and the music hall formed part of the deliberately anti-natural subject matter of the 1890s poets. It is this context also that Horne celebrates in many of his early poems. Mackmurdo's comment that

Horne's work in design was "not so much creative as assimilative" applies equally to the poetry, which at its best remains an
accomplished pastiche of his favourite seventeenth-century
models. Horne had begun his career with translation of Latin
erotic verse by Petronius, Catullus and a poem attributed to
Cornelius Gallus: "Lydia, bella, puella candids."2

At the end of this chapter I have included as much of
Horne's poetry as I can locate. Only a small proportion,
though the best, of Horne's verse was to be published in book
form.[2] His earliest work, dating from 1882 and 1883, shows his
experiments with translations of Latin verse, fragments of
closet drama and humourous occasional verse. "Pictor suae
Amicae Loquitur" dated 9 January 1887 is a Browningesque
monologue, interesting in that it gives expression to Horne's
early antinomianism:

> For as to me, I hold a singular faith
> And do believe that Christ is yet to rise,
> Out of a Hell of custom, church and sect,
> Upon the third day of some coming mind
> To part his Godhead with the Magdalen . . .

We are curiously near Lawrence's "Man Who Died," and the
resurrection of the whole body. An earlier fragment, a closet
drama, has three protagonists, "Ejus, of God," Thur the
Knower, and The Harlot. These represent the complex sides of
Horne's own nature: the frigid, the torrid, and the temptations
of the world and the flesh. The theme is the failure of a promised union of flesh and spirit (the Christ in man) and although
the verse is bad, an ardent mind is clearly at work. The climax
comes when the reviled harlot, idealised by Ejus, breaks his
trance of idealisation:

> Ejus: Easily can I make
>   A gold crown for these sere leaves (crowns her)
>   now indeed,

We are the king and queen of the world and he
Minister to us. Scan him how he is.
All of his notions are night-mare to the earth.
He dare not move, he is kind. Now play the queen—
                                        (thunders)

Hark. Tis the anthem of our coronation—
The sweet psalm of our coronation, sung
By primal intellect of element.
Most golden psalm,—most golden psaltery,
Wherein is gold more golden than thrice purged gold:—
The spirit of gold:—the gold of these sere leaves,—
Of thy dear golden head, thy golden flesh—

Harlot: Ha, ha, sweet sin.

Ejus: Hence, foul and fiendish snake.
       My tears are but manure unto your laughter. (thunders)
       I love you too much to taunt you with my death.
       Remember tho' your eyes see not my blood
       Grow knotted at the temples, as of old
       I do not die—Tho' I am utterly hid
       Awhile, I do not die as others, but I
       Merely forget my sorrows and my flesh.

"Amata Loquitur," published in the *Century Guild Hobby Horse* (1888), recounts how a girl murders her lover, Jeffrey, by strangling him with her wimple, mistaking him for another man, Thwayne, who also loves her and whom she fears and hates. She is discovered by Thwayne who presses her to come away with him and says that he will take the blame for the murder, but she will now be in his power: the weight of guilt becomes heavier each year. The psychology is rudimentary but powerful and another twist is given to the story when the girl escapes from Thwayne and denounces him as a murderer. Thwayne's girdle is found around Jeffrey's neck, but the man himself escapes, and the poem concludes:

> So the pain
> Of these things grows with me, grows for I hear
> The daily tattle call him murderer,
> Who only loved—Loved? Nay, speak Christ! Thou
> knowest,
> Had I but loved as he, Jeffrey had lived.

The casuistry is Browning's, but the tone is melodramatic and resembles such monologues as "Red Bradbury's End" and "Bell in Camp" and Symons's *Days and Nights* (1889).

Pre-Raphaelite influence, according to Loraine Hunt, is readily apparent in Horne's verse, and she cites the careful topographical detail of "Amata Loquitur":

> the hills are high,
> Too high for any wind of earth to bear
> The sound across the rush-pools on the heights,
> The circle of bleached stones, the early way,
> The fallen cromlechs, and the miles of waste . . .
> It is not full time for the Angelus,
> It is not six.

The poem's narrative is sharp and rapid and suggests the influence of William Morris's adaptation of the Sagas in his early romances while the names and the action recall "The Haystack in the Flood." Similarly, Horne's love poetry touches the hieratic, transforms the beloved into an *objet de culte* quite in the Rossettian manner:

> You are the treasure that God
> (O Blessed Lord!)
> Made of gold light and ivory dew . . .
> In that I lodge my soul with *you.*

or again:

> dwell with me as a Psalm—
> Twice sung within the House of Life,—

A sense of personal despair and dissatisfaction—and perhaps also a note of weary idealism—appear in the poems in which Horne seems to be speaking for himself and directly to the reader. This emerges in his complaint of the materialism that results in destroying the architecture of the past or defacing London with buildings, such as those erected in Northumberland Avenue at this time, which are void of all distinction. In general, Horne's poetry is very much that of the earnest young man.[3]

Other fragments, in the archives of the Museo Horne, reflect the influence of Blake and Rossetti, and a further early fragment in octosyllabics gives us an odd mixture of Swinburne's "Atalanta in Calydon" and Milton's Sabrina.

Horne's most distinguished work is in lyric form. What is notable is that he benefited from his association with Arnold Dolmetsch: his lyrics are singable; they fulfill Pound's prescription that one should compose in the sequence of the musical phrase. Their diction is stylish but not conspicuous.

A group of poems entitled *Corona Corinnae*, written in 1887 and published in the *Century Guild Hobby Horse* in 1888, celebrates Horne's admiration for one of the dancers in the Alhambra Ballet of the Season given in that year. The name Corinna is taken from Herrick and one of the poems in the group is addressed to the Caroline poet. With his ideal of "cleanly-wantonness" (in the manner restraint, in the matter exuberance) and his reconciliation of the religious and the sensual in the two parts of his *oeuvre*, *Hesperides* and *His Noble Numbers*, Herrick seems to have become Horne's general model in the later 1880s. In 1887 Horne produced a selection from the poet's work and wrote some carols in dialogue form modelled on Herrick, with an eye perhaps to Parry or Somervell, and on Dolmetsch's seventeenth-century instruments and his ensemble.[4]

In 1891, Horne published a selection from his own poems with the title *Diversi Colores*. This is a small elegant book, with format and typography of his own design. The frontispiece is printed in red and black, the red being used for the flower which occupies the centre of the page and divides the date in roman numerals and the details of publication: "London. Published by the Author at the Chiswick Press." It is doubtful that this lettering, split non-phonetically, altogether satisfies the severe criteria of Horne's later articles on typography and book design. In the copy of *Diversi Colores* at the Museo Horne, there is a note in Horne's hand:

> Seven designs for poems, already written, which I made as a present to Mackmurdo.
> I afterwards altered and engraved some of them intending to have finished a set to publish in book form.
> I had not seen Blake's Songs of Innocence and Experience when I drew the design for the frontispiece and the design for "Complain to Me."

Horne published only three poems after the appearance of his book, one in Rickett and Shannon's *Dial*, one in Headlam's *Church Reformer*, and one in the *Hobby Horse* (1893). Some fragmentary translations from Michelangelo also survive from the late 1890s.[5]

The sadly depleted volumes of English poetry in Horne's library at Florence are an index to his models and aims. Restoration drama and poetry are represented, but the main holdings consist in seventeenth-century poetry and prose, most in contemporary editions. Sir Thomas Browne is prominent; Donne's *Devotions* of 1624 and his *Paradoxes* of 1633 suggest that Horne shared the general nineteenth-century taste for Donne's prose above his verse. Besides the expected figures, including no less than four volumes of Rochester, there are more recondite volumes such as S. P. Gent's *Gestum Voluptatis*

(1639); John Gollop's *Poesis Revidiva* (1656); A. Ross's *Muses'
Interpreter* (1648) and Hunnis's *Hive of Honeysuckles* (1629),
along with several Cavalier anthologies. Though Crashaw and
Marvell are represented in the library, it seems Horne clearly
preferred the Cavalier lyrists above the Metaphysical, though
his own lyrics recall the Elizabethans. Yet those are not precisely pastiche for such assumes another's voice or a personality or personal language. What Horne's lyrics aspire to is
"anonymity," timeless diction. Like his contemporaries of the
Rhymers' Club, he favours long Latin titles, often culled from
the Vulgate and, occasionally, like them, Latin refrains. Some
are faintly Pre-Raphaelite; others are plain and unsentimental,
though in some a hint of a pre-Georgian mode, the sentimental urban pastoral.

A verse from a poem published in the *Century Guild
Hobby Horse* (1891) suggests that his reason for abandoning
verse was not confined to a sense of artistic failure:

> Tell him, that beauty is but lent
> So long as, neither brief desire
> Be quenched through glut, nor yet be spent
> By lack of that, which feeds its fire.

It seems that the area of his experience had somehow con-
tracted, bringing with it perhaps some compensating intensity
in new fields.

AMICO SUO

When on my country walks I go,
    I never am alone:
Though, whom 'twere pleasure then to know,
    Are gone, and you are gone;
From every side discourses flow.

There are rich counsels in the trees,
    And converse in the air;
All magic thoughts in those and these
    And what is sweet and rare;
And everything, that living is.

But most I love the meaner sort,
    For they have voices too;
Yet speak with tongues, that never hurt,
    As ours are apt to do:
The weeds, the grass, the common wort.

UPON RETURNING A SILK HANDKERCHIEF

Winged with my kisses go, go thou to her,
    And bid her bind thee round her faultless throat;
Till thou, close-lying o'er the charmed stir
    Of her white breast, grow warm and seem to float
Away into the golden noon, the still,
    Deep sunlight of her. Oh, sleep on! 'Tis thine,
        Love's summer day. No, not June's thronged hours
So glad are, when the songs of birds fulfil
    Earth, and the breezes in the grass decline,
        Held by the scent of many thousand flowers.

Yet loose that flood of kisses, which thou hast,
    Into her bosom, and through all her hair;
Whispering, it is my utmost wealth amassed
    For her, being fairest; nor do thou forebear,
Until she feel my spirit, like a blush,
    Steal by her shoulder and frail neck; for when
        The gorgeous scarlet, burning, shall have moved
Over her cheek, the little after-hush
    Will tell to her, that I am happy then,
        God! for how short a time, and she is loved.

Loved? Wherefore loved that never, but in thought,
    May be possessed? Is it, that thus might grow
From out a look, a touch, long past to naught,
    My Beatrice, and my perfect love; and so
Dwell with me here, although the while I guess,
    'Tis but a dream, which only does me wrong?
        O wretched truth! and yet the hour, that girds
My pensive nature with her loveliness,
    Would bitter be, as 'tis unto this Song
        To wed these thoughts too stern for dainty words.

Would 'twere no dream, this dream; this long, devout,
    Untiring worship, vainly yet essayed;
This absolute love; then were the torturing doubt,
    The troubled ocean of the soul allayed:
Desire would have her lust, and we have ease,
    Here, from her everlasting thirst; nor pine
        Vainly; but feel the fret, the harrowed breath,
The throbbing heart, that will not, will not cease,
    Stilled into marble, Greek-like, calm, divine,
        Remembering not the past. Stay! This is Death.

MULIEREM EX OMNIBUS NON ENVENI

Of late, a sadness often strays
Here, in my mind: and what besides?
    Within your hair, your face abides;
As summer, through the summer days.

Here do all times, once glad, arise,
    Which now have lost their pleasantness:
    Here dwell the voices of your dress;
Your fragrant ways, your lifted eyes.

Here are all words, you've said; whereof
    Hope never made a tale more dear:
    All, that in Danae showed, is here;
But where is Love?

CEASE, CEASE REPROACHFUL EYES!

Cease, cease reproachful eyes! I have not done
    Aught, that should bring me over this unrest.
Tell me my fault! Have end! Search, one by one,
    All possible errors, which have Time possessed:
I swear you, naught upon me shall you prove;
Unless it be a fault in me to love.

Oh! were you here with me, that I might speak
    No matter what unheeded words, and vain;
I would persuade me, that the look I seek
    Was given: but for me there must remain,
Beneath the one, unalterable guise,
This torture. Nay! Cease, cease; relentless eyes!

CORONA CORINNAE

Being a Celebration, in Six Songs, of a
Masque of Dancing, Named the Seasons.

I. To His Muse, by Way of Prologue

Go! bid Love stay,
   And make a maddening rhyme
     Unto the dancing feet;
     That may perchance repeat,
   Within some other brain, another time,
This measure done, forgotten, put away!

Ah! if it might, might in an hastening year
   Re-woo its magic from the ravening past;
     Make suddenly the movement, the delight,
The gaiety, the freshness, re-appear:
   Although no longer than a thought it last!
       Ah, if it might!

II. Of this Land of Love's

This is Love's land, and here we find
   The birds and flowers, that are his own;
Nothing there is unlike his mind,
   Nothing, but he therein is shown:
For wings, and leaves, and blossoms, prove
Themselves the very heart of Love.

Here are the seasons, that Love's year,
   Nay, that each hour of Love, must know;
Though they the gaudy June do bear,
   They bring him wintry times also:
Still, still, methinks, he would not change;
Though, in their stead, 'twere his to range
Through the deep grass, by flowery roads,
Where gleam the white feet of the Gods.

III. The Measure

Between the pansies and the rye,
Flutters my purple butterfly;

Between her white brow and her chin,
Does Love his fairy wake begin:

By poppy-cups and drifts of heather,
Dances the sun and she together;

But o'er the scarlet of her mouth,
Whence those entreated words come forth,
Love hovers all the live-long day,
And cannot, through its spell, away;
But here, where he was born, must die,
Between the pansies and the rye.

IV. To Herrick

In vain, at all to my content,
Have I my thoughts through nature sent
   To search, with keenest glance,
All things on high, around, below,

But for one figure, that would show
   Corinna in the dance.

Either my brain is dull, or we
With narrow bounds content must be;
   Contented, too, to find
The same sweet flowers, that used to win
The eyes of poets dead, within
   The meadows of the mind:

For only this worn image wrought,
In marble words, the eluding thought
   Justly; and one, I fear,
Familiar as the trees or the sky,
"She dances like my heart, when I
   "Set eyes upon my dear."

Still might I say, as well I could,
When thinking of a summer wood;
   And, truly, one believes
It is the best yet hit upon:
"She dances like the dancing sun,
   "Among the dancing leaves."

But even this, expressing much,
Yet wants, I think, the human touch,
    Which all such styles demand;
For though it laughs upon the wing
Of verse, 'tis but a pretty thing,
    And lacks the master hand.

Ah! Herrick, now where are those rhymes,
Which we in former, thoughtless, times
    And deemed omnipotent
To tell, as never yet was told
In song, all things, which Life of old
    Has unto Beauty lent?

Truly, to thee each joy, that stirs
That secret, wayward, heart of hers,
    Is clay upon the wheel:
These you can fashion as you list;
But not the turning of her wrist,
    The glancing of her heel.

V. "If She Be Made of White and Red"

If she be made of white and red,
As all transcendent beauty shows;
If heaven be blue above her head,
And earth be golden, as she goes:
Nay, then thy deftest words restrain;
Tell not that beauty, it is vain.

If she be filled with love and scorn,
As all divinest natures are;
If 'twixt her lips such words are born,
As can but Heaven or Hell confer:
Bid Love be still, nor ever speak,
Lest he his own rejection seek.

VI. To His Muse in Intercession for Love

Now all be hushed, all, all be wholly still;
For Love is far too glad for song or speech,
Love that hath stayed: now let him have his will;
The mouth, the eyes, the cheek, he did beseech.

Why should he sing? Is it not song enough,
That she, between those sighs that ever start
Suddenly from him, as from Boreas rough,
Should hear the measure from his beating heart?

Therefore constrain him, that he speak no word,
Till the consuming stillness do eclipse
All but delight: then shall no sound be heard,
Save only falling hair, and nestling lips.

Amata loquitur:

Again, O Christ, the bell at Llanagryn!
I heard aright? No, no! the hills are high,
Too high for any wind of earth to bear
The sound across the rush-pools on the heights,
The circle of bleached stones, the early way,
The fallen cromlechs, and the miles of waste:
It cannot be. Yet, hush!—again, twice, thrice.
Fool, that I am! my conscience's in my ears;
It is not full time for the Angelus,
It is not six. And yet 'twas thus I heard
The very sound on Pensarn that foul night
Which makes all days and nights, that follow it,
Terrible as itself; for on that night
I bade Thwane come. 'Twas he alone of man
Or living thing I hated. Well he knew
I loved but Jeffrey, yet he asked my love;
Nor asked it only, but he dogged my steps
And daily made unholy taunts, till he
Seemed like a storm of slander o'er our heads,
Ready to burst, and with a flood of lies
Deluge my love for—nay, 'twas more than love,—
Myself in Jeffrey. Therefore hour by hour
A swift consuming hatred grew in me,
A hatred of his looks, his ways, his words,
Unbearable and restless, and became
Stronger than Love, Love that is strong as Death.
And so I said to him, "Come, Thwane, to-night
Be Ave-bell at nightfall (for it was
Well in the waning of the year); come, Thwane,

To Merlin's seat on Pensarn, half-way up
That silent mountain. Know you it? It hangs
Over the ocean towards Anglesea."
And he replied, "I know it." And I said,
"Thwane, I will give until you ask no more."

Then all that afternoon it seemed the sun
Scarce journied in the heavens, but held the day
The space of many days; and when at length
He past into the sea the hurrying night
Dropt oversoon, like Death, upon the land
And all the ocean. So in haste I sped
Up Pensarn till I reached old Merlin's seat,
And crouched beside it. Then I heard him come
Over the gorse and bracken; and I said
Within myself, "'Tis early that he comes."
And when he came I feigned a stricken voice,
"Hush! speak not for God's sake; someone is near."
And this I feigned, because I inly feared
That if I heard some word that Jeffrey used
Fall from his lips, it might abate my purpose;
So whispered, "Hush!" Nor did I look on him,
Lest seeing he was flesh and blood as we,
I should forget my hatred; so I clenched
My eyes, and drove my soul into my hands
And all my fingers: and I spoke again,
"The night is cold and biting, you shall have
My wimple for a neckcloth." And undid
Quickly my linen wimple from my face
And made a neckcloth. He was looking round,

I think, into the night, perchance to find
The feigned intruder, and scarce heeded he
My words: yet I stayed not for yea or nay,
But threw my linen wimple round his throat
And tied it thus, and thus, and thus; and he
Sank like a sleeping child, down at my feet.
Then knew I I had given as I said,
Nor should he ask again; and so I laughed,
And all the hill-side rang out with my laugh.

Whether it was that I had tied too well
The neckcloth I had made him; or that the night
Grew darker then, so that I could not see
How I had tied the knot; yet this I know,
That, fumbling at the wimple, I had bowed
Myself over his body, and my thoughts
Presently wandered from my fingers, on,
On till I found my eyes held by his eyes.

It was not all at once I knew the truth.
It came not as the bell's sound came just now,
Suddenly, in an instant. It dawned, dawned
Mysteriously and terribly by degrees
Upon my half-numbed sense. It seemed as though
Someone had told it me again, again;
And my poor ears had heard again, again,
What had been told me, but my wretched heart
Dared not to understand it. Yet, at last,
The iron truth broke on me that not Thwane,
Not Thwane—'twas Jeffrey! Then it was I heard
The Angelus ring out from Llanagryn.

It must have been the loosening of the knot
That did release the little dregs of life
From out his lips; for suddenly I caught
A struggling word, as yet I knelt by him
Bowed, like a stone and speechless. Why did he

Speak as he did? He should have cursed me there,
There where I knelt! But no, 'twas not to be;
For his poor heart of grief too soon divined,
From half-said words and broken sentences,
As life came back in waves to ebb again,
Ebb unto death, how he had heard it tost,
For gossip 'twixt the serfs, that I that night
Should meet with Thwane at some appointed place.
But here his soul, as if't had been aware,
Endeavor as it might, it could but speak
Once and begone, shook like a winter leaf
Within its fair-made house of flesh; and he
Strained all his passing breath into these words,
Crying, "I thought to follow unobserved
And find the truth; now have I found the truth.
"'Twas but a snare that you might strangle me?
But I forgive you." Then the thin life went
Up from him like a bubble in a stream.

Whereat my tongue was loosened, and I poured
The bitter, bitter truth into his ears
In vain, for his was dead and heard me not.
But Thou, Christ, Who canst disabuse the soul,
Wilt Thou permit him the in the dismal grave

To say unto his ever-breaking heart,
"Woe! woe! 'twas but a snare to strangle me!"
Still did I pour into his ruthless ears
My own exceeding love for him, my hate
of Thwane; my love, my fear, and my revenge;
Until I knew there stood above my head
A shadow of darkness. And I raised my eyes,
And it was Thwane; and Thwane said, "Even thus
You would have sated me." And so I knew

That nothing of this grief was hid from him.
And Thwane went on, "Now shall you come with me,
Into a place where we shall not be found,
And do my bidding. Come, or I will go
To Hendre telling all that I have seen."
Then I rose up, and with my finger-tips
Smote him upon the mouth, and answered, "Go!"
Yet neither did he go, nor did he make
Me any answer; but from Jeffrey's neck
He took my wimple, and he bound instead
His leathern girdle, and he gave to me
My wimple, crying, "Haste, or I will do
More evil to you than you would. Haste, get
To Hendre, and keep silence; for't shall be,
When they shall find my girdle at his throat,
I shall have past into another land
And in no place be found. Then will they say
Jeffrey by Thwane was killed; but you shall keep
The secret of this evil in your heart,
And day by day its weight shall grow on you,

Till life become as grievous to be borne
As love was sweet."
              Then thought I, "I will go
Swiftly to Hendre, and arouse the serfs;
And they will overtake him on the hills,
And he will suffer what my hate of him
Has brought to pass." So I, without a word,
Turned like a hind to Hendre, and I ran
Into the Hall dishevelled, and in my hand
My wimple, and a lie upon my lips,
Crying, "Lo! I was walking by the beach
And heard a shriek as of a murdered man
Come from the hills towards Pensarn!"
              Then they rose,
Each knight and serf of Hendre, and they searched
Height after height, even until they came
To Cader Idris; yet they found no man,
But only one chill body; and round the neck
Thwane's leathern girdle wound. And so it was,
As he had said, they called him murderer.
But I still keep the secret of these things
Deep in my heart, untold to any man,
For none may understand it. So the pain
Of these things grows with me, grows for I hear
The daily tattle call him murderer,
Who only loved—Loved? Nay, speak Christ! Thou
    knowest,
Had I but loved as he, Jeffrey had lived.

On Certain New Buildings in Covent Garden

O Inigo,
  Could you arise again,
Then men might know
  What sins in stone they chain:

Even in that street
  Where once you did upraise
The calm, discreet
  Sad lesson of your ways.

Was it of old,
  Or is it some new blight,

Men strive for gold
  As you so strove for right?

Her Eyes

Her eyes dwell with me as Psalm—
  Twice sung within the House of Life,—
A Prophet made so glad and calm
  That sometimes when with worship rife,
We learn through its mysterious breath
To hear the voice of God beneath.

Indeed a holy, joyful Song!
  Though those repeated chords are still,
It echoes all the day along
  The laughing ways that skirt the hill;
By meadows that no frosts control
Through all the summer of the soul.

FOR MADONNA OF YESTERDAY—DAISY

Life is young and Love's a maying
Ours the gust of April days
In Love's hour there's no delaying
Time to sigh or time to praise
          What are blisses
          She but kisses
And those warm sweets close confined
Which thus these happy girdles bind.

Time is coming—fires shall robe her
O but hers are too short hours
When shall follow sad October
Those dead leaves of these our flowers
          You must pass by
          As well as I
And the cold earth shall kiss the cheek
Which now my burning lips do seek.

To the Flowers, to Weep

Weep, roses, weep, and straightway shed
                Your purest tears.
Weep, honeysuckles, white and red:
And with you, all those country dears;

Violets, and every bud of blue,
                More blue than skies;
Pinks, cowslips, jasmines, lilies, too,
                Pansies and peonies.

For she, that is the Queen of flowers,
                Though called the least
Lies dropping beneath dreadful Hours,
Megaera has from Hell released.

Weep, till your lovely heads are bent:
                Weep, you, that fill
The meadow-corners; and frequent
All the green margins of the rill.

Flood, flood your cups with crystal tears,
                Until each leaf,
Each flower, through all the upland, wears
The dole and brilliance of your grief,

So that the Lark, who had from Heaven withdrawn,
                Re-sing to you
His song, mistaking noon for dawn,
                And those your tears for dew.

A Song

The wistful wind is weaving
Her whispers o'er the sea;
To lull it, ere her leaving
The waves to tempestry—
Wilt thou not whisper something even to me?

I knew many tempests—
Storms of strange delight,
Storms of sorrow's conquests,
I can still them quite
So that thou whisper something tho' love it blight.

The Bread and the Wine

There were words that our Lord said
The while before he bowed his head
Within the House of Death; and he
Spake these words to the world and thee.
When he had kept the Passover;
And the going forth of the Lord was over:
When he had fulfilled the written Law
That year, as the years before:
He took the wine and took the bread,

And blessing them, 'twas then he said,
"This is my blood, the wine; and this
The bread my very body is.
So it was given to me
That my father might dwell in me,
When the word took the flesh on;
For I and my father are one."
"Little children, if ye love me,
Do this in remembrance of me,
Ever then ye drink and eat
The wine and the meat;
Saying after me,
'This is my blood, the wine; and this
The bread, my very body is.'
With trembling and humility,
Lest ye, eating unworthily—
Not discerning the Lord within
The bread and the wine, do cause, thro' sin,
The honour of God to pass,
And the glory of God as grass."
"Eat, drink then, so that ye may
With love and with works make full the day;
For toil is the prayer of God;
And living this life is the coming of God;
           (presence)
And the love for thy brother the light of God."
"Therefore, if ye love me,
Do this in remembrance of me:
Nor constrain me to depart—
Me and my father from your heart,

By fasting and by abstinence,
By feasting and intemperance."
These were the words that our Lord said
The while before he bowed his head
Within the House of Death. Now he
Spake these words to the World and Thee.

PICTOR SUAE AMICAE LOQUITUR

You call me idle; for, you say, this canvass
Is ten days old and still immaculate.

Yes I have had a score of girls to strip
And scores of studies are the outcome:—one
Has thighs like Titian; another has the breasts
And arms of Michael Angelo: this and this
With some great modern would possess one:—all,
The Harlots, strive to sink one's soul a pander
To what's already done and better done
Than ever I shall do it. But the day,
I had yet to break over the world, nor stoop
To sell her soul for bawdry with the night,
Forestalls no light in them; since they forbid
Me bring out my inner treasury
The new that is so old and yet so new.

For, as to me, I hold a singular faith
And do believe that Christ is yet to rise,
Out of a Hell of custom, church and sect,
Upon the third day of some coming mind
To part his Godhead with the Magdalen.
So it suffices not that whoso gives,
Gives the whole woman in the Magdalen
If she foreshadow not the God. But you—

Whether it is the mistress makes the soul
Or you thro' knowledge have imbibed my nature—
When you release that Paradise of yours
From the strong flaming angels of your dress
There do uprise such possibilities
As must eclipse the soul of Blake himself
And mar the art of Sarto.

As it is
You call me idle. Idle is to you
This extremity of labour. But in truth,
That almost doing the impossible;—
That wondrous fathom of heaven one or two
Exceed above the rest of the low world;—
Those self-conceptions not to be expressed;
These are they which diffuse God through the work
Saving them from Hell—Oblivion;
Even so that they shall never wholly die.
And most I wish *you* should not wholly die.

For I believe the soul alone shall live;
And yet most men possess not soul to live.
For I believe that souls are those white wings
That lift men up into that fathom of heaven;
Which, since the dull world has no faith to see
The blessed sway and flutter of those wings,
Speaks of them as an essence in the mind,
Calling them genius.

Then what soul have you
To raise you out of Death? Thus much have you—
I do believe that whatsoever thing
I touch in genius that shall never die;
So I endeavor that you above all things
Should know that resurrection of my spirit.
And since I wait until the power be come
You only call me idle.

Look you:—this
(Not that way up, the other—don't you see?)
This charcoal "smudge" you call it—is the soul
The Christ that saves the picture or the sketch
In common language. This—better you think?
More to your mind—is right!—I kist it right,
Each limb for limb, each line for line of you:
So like it is the Devil could not mind it.
To me the thing's necessity:—to the world
A picture. (Would to God that all the Lord's
People were prophets; Ah! but who is the Lord's.)
Well both are right and perfect sketch and study.
But still they wait.

Why not begin at once?
Endue the sketch with form and make it glow
With all the rainbow glory of the soul—
An intellectual dinner—nothing more?
More, how much more—more above me to say—
Still more to do: and here, my love they stand
Till God himself shall fuse one in the other.
And yet sometimes I think the spirit comes;
But 'tis as when your hair touches my face
To pass.—And sometimes I'm sure 'tis come:
And I who have been waiting brush in hand
Leap to the canvass, but it is *not* come.
Then all those holy possibilities,
Before my eyes as ghosts, hurry away
Into an everlasting death of shame.
You know not what a night I make of day;
And what a day of night:—how should you know?
And sometimes I grow weary of high aims:—
Seem to myself a traveller that has past
Over the earth again, again; and yet
The line where earth and heaven meet and kiss
Is still far off as ever. So it is:
And still you call me idle, since I wait
For power to fuse the soul and body. Love,
I am content to wait: well—kiss me dear!

LITTLE THINGS

I bring her little things whene'er
I seek the guerdon of the fair
But O would that her love repay
If I could give the world away?

Nay—you whose mouths are filled with scorn
Nay; why was love so lowly born
And Beauty so exceeding clad
With wealth no Croesus ever had.

Had poor love loved in his estate
He had not known the rod of fate
But only held the gentle sway
Which true love feels from day to day.

I bring her little things whene'er
I seek the guerdon of the fair
But O would that her love repay
If I could give the world away?

A COPY FROM CATULLUS

Nay, had but you, most beautiful, most loved,
                    Given me all my way:
Thrown back your gorgeous head out of pure joy,
                    Nor stirred at all, till I
Had with three hundred thousand kisses shut
                    Those honied eyes of yours;
My heart would not have sated been. No, no!
                    Not if our kisses' score
Surpassed the infinite ears of ripened corn,
                    That summer looks upon.

A CAROL FOR CHRISTMAS EVE

We are but of such mortal mould,
  Nos exaudi, Domine!
That the night can scarce withold
  In its shroud our sins from Thee.

That night comes, when Thou shalt come
  Nos exaudi, Domine!
From Thy home to this sad home,
  And die for us upon the tree.

If then the stars shine out so bright,
  Nos exaudi, Domine!
That Thou seest by their light,
  How great our sins and many be;

Thou wilt come, as they were not,
  Nos exaudi, Domine!
Or as they were all forgot,
  Or forgiven, Lord, by Thee.

CHAPTER 4

The Craftsman and Architect

As with his poetry, Horne's work in design tapers off sharply after 1890. In that year, his partnership with Mackmurdo was dissolved. Horne had become, in Mackmurdo's version, too absorbed in his literary work to be much assistance with the firm's architectural commissions, though Horne was to be engaged for a year or two afterwards on one of his own more ambitious buildings.

During the 1880s, Horne seems to have executed a number of designs for the Guild on his own account, and a list in his own hand survives in the archives of the Museo Horne. These include items as diverse as cretonnes, tapestries, chairs, fenders, ecclesiastical chintz, panels for cabinets, pictures in watercolours and oils, wood blocks and a reredos. This again casts some doubt on Mackmurdo's account of Horne's work for the Guild—that it was sparse and that Horne's talent was assimilative, not creative.[1]

Horne's dissatisfaction with his own creative work, and perhaps with the historicism that inhibited it, emerges from the introduction he wrote for his edition of the anonymous play

51

Nero (1624), in a volume of the Mermaid series containing three other plays with introductions by other writers.[2] It can be assumed that the play represented in some measure Horne's own choice. Indeed, both the choice of play and introduction show Horne moving towards a more disciplined, severer taste. *Nero* is an academic play, performed no doubt at the University, written by a scholar and intended for a scholarly audience. It is for a Jacobean play remarkably unified in its design, for it is without any comic element. Plot is rigidly subordinated to historical material. *Nero* lies, then, in the tradition of Jonson's *Sejanus*, a filiation which Horne himself does not observe.

Horne's was not pioneer work. A. H. Bullen had already edited *Nero* from the two extant quartos, but Horne was the first to use the manuscript version. In his reference to the early printed texts, Horne reveals a precision unusual even among more professional editors of that time. The introduction is more interesting as revealing certain pressures at work in Horne's mind than in presenting the background of the play: very often it reads like a personal statement of ideas that possess a merely tangential relationship to the play itself. But this is very different in kind from the subjective approach then in vogue—the approach, for example, followed by Pater's young disciple Arthur Symons, whose editorial work is also represented in the Mermaid volume.[3] In this respect, Horne's introduction may be seen as a remarkably early reaction against the disjunctive method of Lamb's *Specimens*, no less than a veering away from the Paterian approach:

> we of this nineteenth century are, alas! too often content to judge of a
> work of art by fragments, and this is quite an impossible way to judge
> of a work of art, no matter if it be a piece of architecture, a picture, or
> a play.

This strongly hints at tension between the framework of fact and the individual response, a tension felt also in Pater's approach to the Renaissance. In Pater's case this was resolved by turning away from history to fantasy in *Imaginary Portraits* and to the novel in *Marius the Epicurean*. In his *Letters and Papers of Adam Legendre*, which began publication in the *Century Guild Hobby Horse* in 1890, Horne was turning to fantasy of a severer form, but from then on retreated into pure scholarship.

The last act of *Nero*, Horne complains, is comparatively pallid when set beside the other four, for the tragedy expressed in the famous, apocryphal *qualis artifex pereo*, an emperor-aesthete who attempts to modulate politics in the spirit of art, is not emphasised. Horne did not have sufficient knowledge of Elizabethan dramatic conventions to approach the play directly: he does not see that the subdued conclusion to *Nero* is prescribed. What he can do is refer to the historical material out of which this somewhat heavily sententious play is made. In doing so, he proffers an interesting, if obscure, argument, which precisely springs from the misunderstanding of Elizabethan convention:

> History seeks to show us men and events as they really were; while the end of great dramatic writing is not merely to hold the mirror up to Nature, but looking upon Nature to distinguish between what is transitory and what is abiding, what is accidental and what is essential, and so, choosing those qualities and traits of men and women which are the more lasting and precious for our warning and example, and heightening their various passions and circumstances, to mould all into a work of art. If this is so, there would seem to be between History and Dramatic writing a radical contradiction. To say that it is vain that an artist should attempt to hide this contradiction would be an absurdity; for whatever is possible to Art, that also is lawful. Still the question remains, has any writer completely overcome what would seem to be an insuperable objection?

Superficially, this passage re-states the traditional tension between poetry and history found in Aristotle's *Poetics*, but there seems to be some deeper scepticism at work. History with all its morally irrelevant detail is directly related to life; art with its conscious stress on selected morally important detail remains subtly distanced from life. This statement reflects a crisis in Horne's thinking—a dissatisfaction with his own multifariousness.

A similar concern with "architectural" unity appears in a lengthy letter Horne contributed to the *Church Reformer* (March 1888), condemning Bodley and Garner's reredos, recently erected in the chord of the apse of St. Paul's at a cost of close on £30,000. With its statuary, the reredos was barely calculated to satisfy the increasing austerity of Horne's taste.

Horne's analysis of St. Paul's in this article is sensitive and scholarly, yet fails to isolate the Baroque elements; but Baroque was hardly a concept in the architectural criticism of the English 1890s, though Wolfflin's *Renaissance und Barock*, which distinguished the two styles, had appeared in 1888. While he misses the play of solemnity and solidity against dynamic spatial effects in the interior, Horne does isolate Wren's contrast of rectilinear and curved lines. For him, however, the contrast is static. His essay of 1893 on Michelangelo shows him reacting uneasily against violent developments in the Renaissance style.

In 1889 Horne was afforded the opportunity of applying his architectural ideals. A year or two before he had become friendly with Frederic Shields (1833–1911), a friend of Rossetti in his later years (who was to contribute memories of Rossetti to the *Century Guild Hobby Horse*). Since 1883 Shields had been friendly with Mrs. Russell Gurney, a pious and wealthy widow connected with the Quaker banking family. In 1887 Mrs. Gurney decided to build a chapel for rest and meditation to be decorated with symbolic murals by Shields. A site was chosen on the north side of the Bayswater Road: a disused burial ground with an old chapel and a caretaker's house. Horne was appointed architect, and on 1 January 1889 we hear of him visiting the site for the first time with Shields. In the summer of that same year, architect and painter made a tour in Italy at Mrs. Gurney's expense to study some of the principal church decorations, though Horne's role was simply to provide wall-space for Shield's murals. Horne admired particularly the façade of Santa Maria della Grazie at Pietrasanta near Carrara. Saxl has indeed shown that this provides the model for Horne's design.[4]

Mackmurdo lays claim to the Chapel of the Ascension in his autobiographical notes, but a plan of the building in Horne's hand survives in the Victoria and Albert Museum.[5] That Mackmurdo gave some mild assistance is evident from a letter Selwyn Image addressed to him on 26 September 1889:

> I received last night a letter full of commissions from H. P. H. Among them is this which concerns you . . .
> "Will you ask Mackmurdo to do the following:
>   1) Get carefully surveyed all the burial ground, at Hyde Park Place, upon which we are to build the Shields chapel, against my coming home. Particularly, the position of the tombs at the back of the present building. I shall have so very little time to get out my plans, that it is very important that this survey should be taken before I return."[6]

It was not until February 1890, five months later, that the plans were completed. The site was narrow and rendered the more exigent since the tombs, the ante-chapel and the caretaker's house had all to be preserved. Moreover, the site concerned a number of authorities. "Progress was barred," Horne wrote, "by a special Act of Parliament, a Rector, Churchwardens, a Vestry, and a Burial Board; also, if I remember rightly, a Duke and his interests came in, some way or another."[7] The building was finally completed in 1892 and

Shields's decorative scheme was finished in 1894. Like much of Horne's ecclesiastical work, the Chapel suffered in the blitz and has recently been demolished. So far as can be gathered from photographs, there was a beamed roof and some simply designed stalls arranged to face one another across a central aisle in the manner of a College chapel.

Horne's other work in architecture deserves some brief allusion. About 1893, he and Image worked on the interior of Percy Dearmer's Church, St. Anne's Lambeth.[8] A year or two later, Horne added a baptistery and designed furnishings for St. Luke's, Camberwell, which became another war casualty.[9] From plans in the Victoria and Albert Museum, the Baptistery seems to have followed Italian Romanesque models and the design for the bench-ends contains stylized flowers loosely surrounded by streamers. That Horne provided elaborate wall decorations we gather from sketches which are extant.[10] Horne also designed a porch, with a library above, in severe Renaissance idiom for the now demolished Positivist Chapel of Humanity, Chapel Street.

Of his secular work, the most striking designs are High House, at Brook Green, a girls' school, and a house that was never in fact built in Gliddon Road, West Kensington. Both are in late Renaissance style: the Gliddon Road house rather surprisingly presents such Baroque features as a fat swag across the lintel of the front door and a broken pediment on the window immediately above. Horne also designed the new buildings in Brewhouse Court, Eton College; a public house along the Uxbridge Road and some minor domestic work; a house at St. Margaret's; alterations to Mrs. E. L. Vaughan's house, the Marches, Willowbrook, Eton; and a bridge in the year 1891.[11]

Horne seems also to have designed or collaborated with Mackmurdo in the design of the Savoy Hotel.[12] As an architect, he was inclined, like Mackmurdo, to work regardless of cost,

which explains why a number of his buildings never tran-
scended the drawing board.

In October 1889, Mackmurdo purchased 20 Fitzroy Street,
an Adam building of the 1790s, and like most buildings connected with the Guild, destroyed in the war of 1939-1945. The
ground floor was fitted out as workrooms for the Guild. Image,
Horne and the painter T. Hope McLachlan had studios on the
first floor, and Lionel Johnson lived in two rooms on the top
floor between 1890 and 1895.[13]

Henry Sirr has left us a description of the interior at this
period:

> Mackmurdo [had] enlivened its face by white paint on the
> woodwork of windows, door and fanlight, and a number and
> knocker in brass. Window blinds of slight strips slung together
> afforded ventilation besides shade, but he advocated, if not entirely
> closed, nearly closed windows during strong sunlight. An entrant was
> greeted by a circular warm Della Robbia relief let into a wall of the
> white tinted vestibule. An imposing Italian painting of fine colouring
> in [the] original frame overspread the width of the projecting breast
> above the mantel in the drawing office adjoining, this space after-
> wards well filled by a Selwyn Image cartoon. Happy colouring of the
> wall covering secured brightness for two large rooms which could be
> thrown into one on the first floor, enhanced by lustre of his fitments,
> brass wall sconces and hanging candelabra, and long low mantel
> mirror with reflecting facets in richly gilded framework. Opportunity
> was not missed for an inscription of excellent lettering on the front of
> a fixed cupboard in the cream coloured refectory below the drawing
> office.
>
> Dullness was absent, disposal of furniture was discriminating and
> airiness prevailed.[14]

The house was called "Whiteladies," though known more
generally to two generations as "The Fitzroy Settlement." (It
was from here, as well as from Mackmurdo's office at 28

Southampton Street, Strand, that the *Century Guild Hobby Horse* was edited).

Sirr recalls for us the personages who frequented 20 Fitzroy Street in the 1890s, many of them contributors to the Guild's magazine: Dowson being lighted downstairs in the early hours by Lionel Johnson, both missing their footing and landing in a scurry of broken glass at the bottom of the steps; Johnson creeping like a spider up the ninety-seven steps to his rooms; Sturge Moore, looking with his flowing beard like one of the apostles, reciting verse to the zither; Yeats declaiming. Sickert, Crane, Augustus John, Rothenstein, Jepson, Rhys, Wilde, Symons: hardly a representative figure of the decade is missing from the list of those who at one time or another were entertained by conversation, poetry reading—the meetings here developed into the slightly less informal Rhymers' Club— and the concerts under the direction of Dolmetsch. From records in the Dolmetsch archives at Haslemere, it can be gathered that five concerts were held at 20 Fitzroy Street between 19 December 1891 and May 1892. Horne was deeply interested in early music and instruments and this interest is reflected in the *Century Guild Hobby Horse*. Helen Combe, who decorated Dolmetsch's "green" harpsichord, and was later to marry Roger Fry, was a frequent visitor. So too was Fry himself. His Omega Workshops were to prolong in somewhat different form the ideals of the Century Guild into the twentieth century.

CHAPTER 5

Crucial Years as Editor

Such notice as Horne occasionally receives from literary historians derives from his association with the *Century Guild Hobby Horse* (5.1). After some feeble contributions to the first, abortive issue of 1884, Horne edited all the later issues from 1886 to 1891. For this stylish quarto, he not merely superintended and contributed largely to the letterpress, he also designed initials and tailpieces (5.2) and prolonged Mackmurdo's policy of using handmade paper, Caslon type and Chiswick Press printing. Emery Walker became responsible for the reproduction of drawings and other graphic work, all of which is of high quality. As Aymer Vallance remarked, "never before had modern printing been treated as a serious art, whose province was to embrace the whole process, from the selection and spacing of the type and the position of the printed matter on the page, to the embellishment of the book with appropriate initials and other decorative adornments."[1] Indeed, there are hints of an ideal unfolding of content, of issues subtly planned as a unity.

The allegiances of the magazine were in matters of theory to Ruskin and Morris, but in artistic practice to Blake, the Pre-Raphaelites and Simeon Solomon. Rossetti, Madox Brown, James Smetham and others figure prominently with the accent

fig. 5.1 *Century Guild Hobby Horse*, cover page.

THE CENTURY
GUILD
HOBBY HORSE.

IT is our intention early in the new year to issue our first number of the "CENTURY GUILD" periodical; a literary work issued at fixed price, though not at fixed intervals, the object of the periodical precluding. For our sole motive in publishing anything at all, is the desire to meet the call that comes from some few friends, sharing our views, and interested in our exercise of the arts, to share likewise our thoughts, which by virtue of this sympathy or personal friendship are in correctness and by courtesy theirs.

Further, for extended enjoyment, we desire to give in some form, other than that of our special craft, articulate and permanent expression to what seem to us some of the finer

fig. 5.2 *Century Guild Hobby Horse*, tailpiece and "C" designs

on fugitive and unpublished material: Horne's archival instinct stirred early. Blake's *Marriage of Heaven and Hell* was printed in ordinary type in the issue of October 1887. Horne's intention was that "now for the first time it will be possible for the many students of Blake, to whom the few original, and the scarcely more plentiful facsimile copies are inaccessible, to judge of it as a whole, and form some estimate of its worth as a prose work apart from the decorative designs in which it was set by Blåke."[2] Horne proceeds to inform the audience about the text, explaining that the transcript he used was first collated with an original copy in the Fitzwilliam Museum, Cambridge. The few emendations are noted. Although he altered some of Blake's punctuation to aid sense, wherever possible Horne preserved it "and invariably his spelling, notwithstanding its errors; for the trivial faults of some men have more interest and distinction than the virtues of half the world."[3]

In July 1890, the *Century Guild Hobby Horse* printed for the first time Blake's *Book of Los.* Frederick York Powell, friend of John Butler and W. B. Yeats, found Blake's copy of this book dated 1795 and he explains in a note that this piece "lay for some time in the British Museum. It was not mentioned in the catalogue of Blake's works, affixed to the first edition of Gilchrist's excellent life of Blake, 1863." The significance of the *Book of Los,* according to Powell, is that along with "*Ahania, Urizen,* and probably the lost *Oothoon,* [it] reveals Blake's mystic Cosmogony and Mythology. . . . I first read and wrote out this poem in December 1874 from the British Museum copy, the only one known to me."[4] A rare broadsheet illustrated and engraved by William Blake to accompany "Little Tom the Sailor," a ballad written by Blake's friend William Hayley, was also printed in the first issue of the *Century Guild Hobby Horse* for 1886 with a note by H. H. Gilchrist.

Horne's mentors for the magazine from 1886 were Lionel Johnson and Arthur Galton (1852–1921)—the latter once a Catholic priest, later at Oxford preliminary taking Anglican orders. Image, however, continued to exert influence on the magazine's direction. Galton, surely a faded name in our time, had some mild reputation as a historian with very decided views of a neo-classical and Arnoldian cast. Indeed, through Johnson and Galton, Arnold also became a presence. Galton consistently wrote essays to sway Horne's inward polemicising against the decline of standards in literature and literary reviewing, exemplified by such non-University men of letters as William Sharp and Edmund Gosse.

As early as 1886, the emphasis of the Guild and its periodical on early English music was anticipated by a piece on Arne. This was not peculiarly pioneering in view of the existence, for example, of the Purcell Society. Other concerns in the earlier issues include the revival of wood cut and the hand arts, a polemic against Impressionism in painting, conceived as Naturalist (as the earlier Impressionists themselves conceived it) and, at the far extreme, against the Royal Society for its exclusiveness. Other interests concern oil painting to the detriment of other arts, the refusal to admit "advanced" art and its betrayal of its teaching role.

The issues of 1886 to 1891 are notable also for Horne's architectural enthusiasms: severity and repose, those seventeenth-century accents he derived from Mackmurdo. Horne was as involved as were Mackmurdo and Image in the principle of "unity of arts"—the ground of polemic against the Royal Society—while Image in his various contributions to the *Century Guild Hobby Horse* stressed not merely music, but acting, literature and the dance as aspects of such unity.

Perhaps Horne's clearest expression of this principle may be gathered from the paper which he read to the students of the Whitechapel Craft School in April 1891 and which was printed in the July 1891 issue of the *Century Guild Hobby Horse*. Defining his terms, Horne states early on in this paper that "I use the word 'Art' in its widest signification, to include Literature, Music, Painting, Architecture; in short, whatever Art is fine in its nature, in contradistinction to those which are merely mechanical." It is a distinction that is found in the Renaissance. From that period too derives the statement that "there are not *many* Arts. As there is but one proper study of mankind, which is man; so there is but one art; the art of a fine and various expression of the human spirit, *multipartite sed indivisibilis*, of many forms, no doubt, but ever impossible to divide." And refuting objections such as "I am concerned only with cabinet making," or "I only with modelling: and what has modelling, or cabinet making to do with literature, or with music?" Horne returns:

> Little or nothing . . . if you consider the furniture, which is commonly sold in our shops, or the carving, which overloads the front of the last new restaurant in the town, to be the models of all that is excellent in Art. But the glazed ware of Della Robbia, and the woodwork of D'Agnolo, are they of this order? Not altogether, I imagine. The practical business of many of those inimitable workmen in Italy, during the 15th and 16th centuries, consisted in some one particular craft, such as you yourselves are practicing: but their interest and concern lay with the whole range of diapason of Art. Go to one of our great Museums, and look at the furniture, the pottery, the metal-work, common articles of daily use, which these men produced: how some figure on a door-knocker will betray their love of antique statuary; some inlaid design on a cabinet, their delight in the poets; some moulding on a candlestick, their study of the Masters in Architecture![5]

Loraine Hunt observes that "it is safe to say that every contributor to the *Hobby Horse* shared Horne's prejudice against 'popular' art and, like him, urged a return to the past for models worthy of emulation. Some advocated going back as far in time as ancient Greece; others recommended the Medieval period or the Renaissance; and a few were satisfied with retreating only to the years before the Industrial Revolution. All, however, agreed that contemporary art—plastic, pictorial, and graphic—was inferior to that of a past time."[6] Certainly, the associated sensibility in an associated society was as much a dream of the Aesthetes as of twentieth-century literary critics.

Architects were advised by Horne to take Inigo Jones as a model:

> He has commonly been accused of studying . . . buildings for the sake of archaeology: he studied them because he knew they would give him Form and Style: and the causes of them, Selection, Composition, Concentration, and Subordination. These make Art, Art; and the possession of them are her essential conditions. . . . Inigo Jones, unlike the architects of recent times, did not clamour perpetually after an architectural style of his own, because he knew that locked in the "hushed casket" of his soul was the magic secret of all architectural style, charm and distinction; not the charm that holds the passing hour of fashion, but that which enchants all time. . . . You [modern architects] think to redeem your failure by the wonder of your appliances. Perchance, unhappily, one day it will dawn upon you, that yours is no failure of not understanding building, but of not understanding life. This Inigo Jones assuredly understood. . . .[7]

In the issues of 1887 we encounter the early twinges of decadence. Two sonnets by John Addington Symonds on Narcissus and Baldur treat their subjects in the manner that might be expected from that lover of blue-breeched gondoliers not as yet at rest "in Aretino's bosom." Horne's continued enthusiasm for Symonds (whose studies in the Italian Renaissance were of course relevant) and later for Dowson was supported by Johnson, while Johnson and Image also shared Horne's early enthusiasm for Pater.

Pater indeed was approached by Horne for the contribution, but the offer was politely declined on the plea of pressure of work. Image and Johnson both reviewed volumes of Pater for the periodical. Horne's increasing preoccupation with book production and the antiquarian, moreover, were marked by contributions from Alfred W. Pollard on old title-pages and later on Greek types. (Image, in fact, designed a distinguished type for this mode.)

By 1888 the magazine, after a faltering start, had established a respected identity. Yet at this point it seems to have suffered a crisis of fortunes. Probably that was as much financial as editorial, though Galton continuously admonished and encouraged Horne, much to Horne's exasperation. During this period, Galton indeed was writing several letters a week full of angry pomp, baroque patronage and scowling pedantry. We learn of the crisis through one of Galton's letters dated 22 April 1888, though only one side of the correspondence survives. The publisher of the *Century Guild Hobby Horse*, Kegan Paul, was involved. Some notes on sales and a cost in Horne's hand, preserved in the archive of the Museo Horne, Florence, remain suggestive:

Cost of No. IX

Kegan Paul for printing etc.	25.	6.	9.
Paper	15.	12.	0.
Illustration on the average	17.	0.	0.

Sales of No.	VII	307
	VIII	277
	IX	287
	X	271

Sales of 600 to July cover costs (100)[8]

This covers the period from April 1887 to January 1888. According to the records of the Museo Horne, sales did not improve until April 1888. In a letter to Lilian Block, Mackmurdo stated that "the *Hobby Horse* was sold only to annual subscribers; it never quite reached 500 subscribers."[9] This is a more robust figure certainly than Horne records. A letter from Lionel Johnson to Campbell Dodgson indicates that the situation continued to cause concern: "By the way, they are financially in a perilous way: of your charity, take in the Hobby Horse! ten shillings a year! do!"[10]

The immediate outcome of the crisis (we may compare the case of the *Germ*) was an agonising reappraisal of the title. Although Galton, Gladstone and others expressed opinions (Galton surely expressed them at great length) and canvassed various names—Prospero, Hesperia, Atlantis, Pallas, Palladium and Saturnia, to say nothing of Formosa—the original title was preserved, even if there were now few references to the Guild from which the periodical had derived its origin and which it had been intended to publicize.

Another editorial crisis smouldered between January and March 1889. The participants were Horne and Galton, with Johnson mediating. The precise cause of the dispute was Galton's essay on William Sharp, which violated Horne's notion that individuals should not be attacked, though the essay actually appeared later that same year in muted form. Horne's position is Paterian in its evasion of raw polemic. One criticises by implication or omission. Galton, moreover, was void of his master Arnold's delicate ironies. Writing on 18 March 1889, Johnson attempted to excuse the angry pomp of Galton's letters to Horne:

> I will only say that Galton is not as other men are, in all ways. When he disputes, controverts, contends, it must be in a "fine last century manner," which implies a certain stately plain speaking with every regard for the felicities of style, and none for the feelings of an opponent.[11]

In the autumn of 1889, Horne was absent in Italy, assembling notions for his Chapel of the Ascension shortly to be built in Bayswater. Image was therefore largely responsible for the preparation of the October issue, though working to a schedule prepared by Horne. The July issue, besides being heavily laced with Pre-Raphaelitism, had also included two illustrations from the *Hyperotomachia*. This work with its bizarre and exquisite images was to influence the book design and illustration of the 1890s, Charles Ricketts particularly. The central article is by Pollard on Geoffrey Tory, "Scholar, Printer and Engraver." A finely printed reproduction of Tory's *Book of Hours* and rubricated letter headings accompany it. Pollard comments on the inadvisability of complex symbolism in book design, stressing instead single type and visible clarity, both criteria of Horne's and Image's book designs in the 1890s and later of Horne's own book on design, though not of certain work of Ricketts, or Wilde's *The House of Pomegranates*. However, the "Contemporary Notes" in this issue contain a warm notice of the first issue of the *Dial*. Image's discussion of Renaissance printers, such as Aldine, Basile and Plantine, is somewhat belletristic in comparison with Pollard's piece, but remains notable for insisting on the notion of total beauty in the book: binding, paper, printing, capitals, and adornments.

In the October 1890 issue, the decadent note becomes more pronounced. Its most substantial exemplar is J. A. Symonds's translation of Bion's pastoral elegy, the "Lament for Adonis," with which Horne assisted considerably. The metre is a twelve to fifteen-syllabled line with unrhymed feminine endings to suggest the hexameters of the original, while a subdued alliteration runs through in compensation for the absence of strict quantity. The most felt passages relate to the description of Adonis's beauty in death. Johnson approved both of the issue and of Symonds's version. And well he might, for to that same issue he contributed a poem, "In Praise of Youth," "which touches, I trust, with delicacy upon Greek virtue and Greek voce. Have you seen Symonds's article on Platonic Love? It is barely decent: the man is an absolute

Priapus, a very Satyr."[12] The allusion is to a piece in the *Artist and Journal of Home Culture,* still pursuing its discreetly antinomian course under Charles Kains-Jackson. Both Johnson and Symonds subscribed to the important (but rationalizing) distinction between Uranian (non-physical) and Pandemian homosexuality, though in Symonds's case that ideal was mostly observed in the breach.

The ideal might refer to an ascending ladder of love, from sight of the beloved to union with the spiritual beauty of the One, but this notion could be readily used as a rhetoric of seduction, a process down the ladder of love from sight to touch and taste. The point is made in a poem by Percy L. Osborn, "Echelle D'Eros," contributed to the *Spirit Lamp,*[13] where the last step of the ladder is described as

> l'union complete;
> L'extase des corps et des coeurs,
> Et je ne sais quelles langueurs.

Alfred Douglas, the editor, described one of Osborn's poems as charming and observed of another: "if ever I feel an inclination to make a short sojourn in one of Her Majesty's jails, I shall seize the opportunity of printing it." And in the upshot, Douglas seems to have seized the opportunity. It was all a question of tone, and the *Spirit Lamp* was an Oxford periodical in an Oxford distinctly secularised and now accustomed to the language of the "new chivalry."

By 1877 long past were the days of the Oxford Professorship of Poetry, when the forces of tradition rallied against the "English Decandents," Pater and Symonds and the Aesthetes. Symonds in the first edition of his *Studies in the Greek Poets* (1876) had lingered over the love of Achilles and Patroclus, praised the Dorians, had distinguished Uranian Love from the celebration of mere *instrumenta libidinis* and organized a not specially convincing attitude to Strato's *Musa Puerilils.* The

sharp reaction of 1877, however, had forced him, no less than
Pater, not merely into revision, but into omission for later
editions. Johnson's poem is more discreet, though less so than
the version later published in *Poems* (1895) and with some
irony dedicated to Alfred Douglas. (The dedication was pru-
dently omitted in the collected edition of Johnson's poems
published in 1915.) There are references, suitably generalised,
to "full lips" and "shapely limbs"; but the young men of the
poem are, like a clutch of Hippolytuses, athletic and pious,
even though their religion seems to owe more to St. Aloysius,
Oxford, than to any Attic fane. It is their aristocratic distance as
well as accessible visual beauty that makes possible a progress
up the ladder of love, though not of course for those not "up"
at the University. Their glimpses sting only the lower passion:

> To be their friend, the common throng
> Would dare all bounds of right and wrong . . .
> But vain! In no unlovely pride,
> They hold together, side by side.

At night, in the sole stanza not muffled by delicacy,

> Almost the murmuring sea is hushed:
> Their eye on fire, their bright limbs flushed,
> They dominate the night with love:
> While the stars burn and flash above,
> These kindle through the dark such flame,
> As if not seen, and hath no name:
> Can night bear more? Can nature bend
> In benediction without end,
> Over this love of friend for friend?[14]

The namelessness of this passion recalls Lord Alfred
Douglas's poem "Two Loves," contributed in 1894 to the
Chameleon which tells of "The love that dare not speak its
name."

Mackmurdo returned as a contributor to the issue of October 1890, with a review article on Charles Herbert Moore's *Development and Character of Gothic Architecture*, a piece exhibiting some uncontrolled *kulturgechichte*. Johnson was supercilious about the author's prose in a letter to Galton:

> Mackmurdo is wonderful: the incomprehensible jargon of aesthetics and positivist dogma; the torrent of abstract nouns, and incongruous adjectives; the formless, ill-sounding and illiterate sentences; all this is marvelous, and, like the piece of God, it passeth all understanding. Beautiful words like "figuration" and "climatical" flourish upon every page.[15]

Granting that Mackmurdo's style was sometimes clumsy, this is occasionally a consequence of attempting to say rather more than his Oxford censors. To this issue Horne offered a review of a new edition of the *Lyrical Ballads*, where the "Thorn" and the lines on "Tintern Abbey" are isolated as Wordsworth's most powerful contributions: the poles certainly of that volume.

The issue of January 1891 appeared a month late, but was highly distinguished. The contents confirm what the "decadent" contributions had suggested, that the mood of the 1890s was being established. The frontispiece was an uncharacteristic painting by Watts entitled *A Roman Lady in the Decadence of the Empire*. Additionally Ernest Dowson contributed for the first time and Johnson furnishes a poem in early Christian Latin, a species of verse and language popular among *fin de siècle* authors.

In his note on Watts's painting, Horne stressed the classicizing of the theme. He used the Arnoldian vocabulary of Attic, Asiatic and Corinthian, though at the same time he alluded to Reynolds's distinction in the *Discourses* between the ornamental in Renaissance painting (the Venetian) and the grandly simple (the Roman). The painting is as usual the starting point of an excursus on the state of present-day art and the necessity for principles of order and unity. There are architectural accessories to Watts's painting, and this allows Horne to generalise: architecture provides the closest index to the "spirit of the Age" and the late nineteenth century is flagrantly Corinthian in its insistence on accumulating the greatest amount of detail in every available space. The argument then returns to Reynolds and veers away from the simple Pre-Raphaelite rejection of Academic Art, whether Raphael or the art of those eclectic painters, like the Carracci, who tried to combine in their work the various excellencies of the sixteenth century. The earlier sixteenth century itself, the Roman Renaissance, was by no means effetely conventional; it was more Attic than we imagine. Indeed, will later generations not find in it more human interest and less sentimentality? There is a nineteenth-century classicism that remains entirely human, entirely natural while still preserving the grand manner. Wordsworth's *Laodamia* is cited here, and thus more rapid shifts from one art to another.

True, nineteenth-century classicism consists in a sophisticatedly harmonious relationship of part to whole. And all this we have heard before; it seems an oddly oblique way of discussing the painting, though the reproduction helps one pass from general to particular. Watts's success in this painting, according to Horne, lies in "the freshness of its form, and the harmony of its masses." Watts has concentrated simply on pose and gesture; there is little ornament, no elaborate detail (such as we should find in the archeological realism of Edward Poynter or Lawrence Alma-Tadema).

Horne's obituary appreciation of Bell Scott, if too indulgent, too much the act of piety, is full at least of information. Some criticism may be involved in the opening generalisation about the Scots as typical Northerners taking rather to intellectual speculation than to sensual impression and being more concerned with the elaboratation of conception than utterance. Horne's emphasis falls on Scott's versatility as painter, engraver, book-illustrator, collector of prints, art historian, poet and, in a loose sense, philosopher. Scott's early familiarity with Blake is glanced at and this leads to his catalogue of Blake's paintings and his etchings after Blake's designs.

Horne's remarks on Scott's verse and his relation to Rossetti are interesting. The firmest characteristic of the verse, the macabre, is peculiarly Northern. This when united with some tincture of Blake produces Scott's finest lyric, "Memory," a rather pallid little poem, but with the unpretentious elegance that might be expected to appeal to Horne. Horne does not scruple to refer to Scott's "genius"—using the word presumably in the sense of his *vis* or gift of personality—but is more objective when he asks us to remember the state of taste when Scott was developing his gift: "In judging Mr. Scott, we must always remember to what generation he belonged; and what manner of men came after him, and were influenced by him. They had the advantage of his propositions, and their's was the profit."[16] Horne also has to stabilize the definition of Pre-Raphaelite: Scott he sees as conforming to Ruskin's definition, "the portrayal of Nature as it was around them, with the help of modern science." If this is a comprehensive definition of the Pre-Raphaelite aim, much that was popularly attributed to the movement, Horne argues, was partially its outcome. Such a definition would, if rigidly applied, include Madox Brown, but almost entirely exclude Rossetti.

Johnson's poem, honouring the Elizabethan Catholic Martyrs of Winchester, is written in five-line stanzas of acatalectic iambic dimeter, rhyming *aabb*. This is a metre common to the earlier Christian poets (Ambroise d'Evreux, Sedulius Scottus, and Venantius Fortunatus) in whom, however, it remains predominantly quantitative rather than accentual. In Remy de Gourmont's words, Saint Ambrose is regarded as having deliberately "disregarded the Horatian principle and so marking the birth of a new mentality."

Of course such interest in early medieval Latin poetry is very characteristic of the 1880s and 1890s. It extended both to criticism and to actual attempts at revival. The immediately influential statements are French. The hero of Huysmans's *A Rebours* (1884) has a cult of early Christian Latin poetry. This is picked up by the hero of George Moore's *A Mere Accident* (1887) and finds a more scholarly vent in Remy de Gourmont's *Latin Mystique* (1892). Early Christian poetry is closely connected with the idea of Decadence. Historical consciousness in the nineteenth century had led to both English and French writers finding parallels between late antiquity and their own age. In France, this occurs (polemically) as early as the 1830s in the criticism of Désiré Nisard. *Marius the Epicurean* (1885) is an English example. Gradually, however, the definition of Decadence seems to veer away from any conception of Empires falling through political and moral corruption: literary decadence begins to be viewed as innovation, as renewal almost, rather than decay. When John Butler Yeats called the poets of his son's time "a generation of Hamlets" he may well have had in mind a view of Hamlet as sacrificial victim, as scapegoat. The point here is that as the *Century Guild Hobby Horse* begins to become open to *fin de siècle* influences, the appearance of an early Christian type of Latin poem altogether symptomatic.

Johnson's poem is, for example, at once a glorification of the Wykehamist Martyrs of the English Reformation and of the Virgin Mary. The poem's central image is probably that fine medieval statue of the Virgin crowned, the holy child in her arms, which still survives in the niche above the outer gate of the school. It is not the most successful of Johnson's Latin poems and the innocent reader is hardly likely to respond to parochial puns, such as

> Quam dulce nomen personat
> Domous! et nostra superat
> Domus terrestres caeteras:
> O domus dulcis! floreas.[17]

The reference is to the monastic origin of the College of St. Mary of Winchester and to one of the school songs. The poem is in the form of a prayer to the three martyrs, who include the famous Father Garnet. The theme consists in a contrast between the earthly and redeemable city of Winchester and the Heavenly City where the Martyrs live, protectors and intercessors.

Dowson's casuistical *A Case of Conscience* has all the characteristics of his short stories: the present is rarely held in bold relief; a mood is evoked rather than a narrative presented; a set of impressions which confirm the notion that the will is either powerless to affect their course, and if asserted is disastrous. *A Case of Conscience* is as usual semi-biographical with its drifting hero's love for a girl-child who is innocent and inaccessible. The finical punctuation and syntax notable in Galton, Image and Johnson is prolonged to its extreme in Dowson. Johnson's "A Note Upon the Practice and Theory of Verse at the Present Time Obtaining in France" has at its aim discussion of "the schools, to which belong, not it may be thought too happily, the names of *decadence* or of *symbolisme.*" Johnson's summary is admittedly based on those of the French critic Anton Lange, and the range involves Wagner and colour-audition. Symbolism itself is defined as "a recognition in things of a double-significance, not the mere natural fact, but the thing as it is in thought."[18] The definition might satisfy Image's criterion of imaginative art, but all mention of vertical correspondences is omitted, and lateral correspondences are only touched on to the degree cited by Lange.

The dialectical relation of symbolism to decadence and naturalism is not boldly defined as it was to be in Symons's article in *Harper's Magazine* of 1893, nor is the importance of Schopenhauer's influence recognised. The drift of the article is towards the familiar polemic against "the vague and vicious talk about the arts, in which the terms of one are misapplied to the other." The oddest omission is Blake, who must have been in Johnson's mind about this time since he was lending some mild assistance to Yeats and Ellis in their elaborate wrestlings with Blake's "symbolic system." Shannon, who had edited the first issue of the *Dial*, contributed to this issue a frontispiece which Johnson "disliked furiously," perhaps as a pallid study of a nude but more likely because of its quasi-impressionist origins: "Its technical excellence, I am told, is great; but that is nothing, without the fine interest, and the charming dignity possessed by all true works of art."[19]

"The Hobby Horse is, for once, on its way to a speedy publication: a good number, but most indecent. Mackmurdo [*sic*] has written another monstrous article, for July," so wrote Johnson to Galton on 5 April 1891. The indecency is barely dramatic: the disquiet of Galton seeing himself in the glass. The classical and austere were always at war with the decadent Johnson. The two contributions which prompted his comment were Shannon's illustration based in approved 1890s style on the Vulgate version of the *Song of Songs* VII.2 and Dowson's famous *Non Sum Qualis Eram Bonae Sub Regno Cynarae*. Dowson was himself dubious about its reception. "It looks less indecent in print," he wrote to a friend while passing proof of the poem, "but I am still nervous! though I admire Horne's audacity."[20] Certainly the torrid matter and the control of metre fulfill Horne's prescription for art.

Johnson, as his poem "Upon a Drawing" indicates, would have found Simeon Solomon's androgynous Bacchus used as frontispiece to the July number more to his taste. It has been visited with high praise by Pater in the first edition of *The Renaissance* and is now in the Birmingham Art Gallery. Galton, like Johnson, frequently agonised about the decadent tone of the *Hobby Horse*: "Will not the frontispiece be thought lewd?"[21]

Horne's article on Edward Calvert was precipitated by the recent life of Calvert by his son, in addition to acquisitions by the British Museum. The article reaffirms the importance of Blake and his "visionary" disciples, no less than Millet, for the Century Guild circle, for those later connected with the *Dial* and the *Pageant*, and later for W. B. Yeats, though Gustave Moreau was still to be added to the canon. Calvert, like Blake's other, more talented disciples, did not imitate the master; indeed Calvert and the others concentrated on landscape painting, an area in which Blake was at his least typical, though later Blake's influence on Calvert extended to engravings on copper, wood and stone. Not imitations, but full of the "spirit" of Blake, Horne found Calvert's landscapes more mysterious and sensuous than those of Blake: the "devout and curious expression of a spiritual theme, by the means of sensuous images,"[22] a definition of a distinctly symbolist tinge.

Horne's second contribution, a paper read to art students of the Whitechapel Craft School, stresses familiar themes: the heresy of progress in the arts; the corruptness of modern taste; the importance of tradition; the affirmation that Art embraces the arts of design. Johnson's piece on French verse is reinforced by two chansons by Gustave Khan in irregularly rhymed verse: "very musical and very misty," so Johnson terms them.

In the October 1891 number, Johnson discusses Robert Bridges, predictably approved of by the Guild, though not without reservation. The stress lies on Bridges's capacity, like the Elizabethans, to write for music. The contrast is with the many modern lyrists of the "wandering cry," those "who go up into the mountain to weep or rage rather than to pray." Symonds discusses a Tiepolo altar-piece; but the most distinguished contributions are Dowson's three poems: "Fleur de la Lune," "The Carmelite Nuns of the Perpetual Adoration" and "Amore Umbratilis."

The dominant article in this issue is, however, Alfred W. Pollard's "Some Remarks on the History of Greek Types, and Upon the Reasons of Their General Lack of Beauty." Pollard argues that the farther "we depart from the Greek manuscripts of the fifteenth century and the nearer we approach to those of the tenth, the more likely are we to find the beauty of form . . . Greek printing has hitherto so signally failed to attain."[23] Pollard includes in illustration several examples of Greek type and manuscript along with a few lines penned by Image which Pollard considers in many respects ideal. Image had independently acted on a theory similar to Pollard's in basing his own script on tenth-century prototypes and was approached a few months later by Macmillan's with a view to designing a new font of Greek of which specimens were to be given in the *Hobby Horse* (1894).

Altogether this issue maintained a good standard, but at the close of 1891 Horne was superseded as editor. In November, Johnson informed Galton

> that unfortunate paper . . . has passed out of Horne's hands, and Mackmurdo is, technically and financially, sole editor and proprietor; but one half of the paper will always be literary, under the informal management of Image and myself. Since neither of us was willing to take the responsibility of becoming editor this plan seemed the best; but I do not prophesy long life to the Hobby Horse under so vague a scheme.[24]

Galton's reaction to Mackmurdo's assumption of control was distinctly negative and he tried to persuade Horne to continue to act, but Horne and Mackmurdo had by this time quarrelled definitively.

The general standard of the January 1892 issue was certainly lower than that of its immediate predecessors and Barclay Squire, the musicologist, wrote to Horne: "What a falling-off in the Hobby Horse since you left! I shouldn't think it would live a year if the other numbers are like the first: 10 p.—though cheap under your editorship—is dear when one only gets bad punctuation for one's money."[25] William Morris was the most distinguished of the contributors, with a reprint of his lecture on "The Influence of Building Materials on Architecture." Like the early issues of 1886–1887, the 1892 volume stresses the Guild's allegiances with the Arts and Crafts rather than the scholarly and "modern" literary contributions readers had come to expect under Horne's direction.

The circle of contributors to the January and the two other issues of 1892 was certainly wider and certainly less distinguished than formerly. Two members of the Rhymers' Club, Le Gallienne and Ernest Rhys, appear for the first time, along with Dollie Radford, the wife of another member. But Horne's interests were still represented in the 1892 volume (though they were Images's also). *A New Poet* by Charles Sayle (a friend of Lionel Johnson) celebrates the "Uranian" sonnets of John Gambril Nicholson, though Sayle polemically finds them "natural" and "healthy." Anthony Deane's article was occasioned by a police raid on an exhibition of paintings illustrating Rabelais. Pressure had been applied by the Purity League and its secretary, the Reverend Joseph Parker, was referred to by Dowson as "that greasy pestilential fellow." Parker was noted for his moral opposition to the theatre and Deane, like Image and Horne, was violently opposed to the Purity League. This issue was to be the last with which Mackmurdo had any connection.

Early in 1893, Elkin Mathews and John Lane issued a
circular for prospective subscribers to a new series of the
Century Guild Hobby Horse. The magazine was to continue in
quarterly numbers and the price was to be one pound in order
to "publish what was formerly issued in half-private manner,
and without regard to loss." The *Studio* carried a similar
announcement.

The first number of this new series appeared early in
1893, printed by Folkard and Son and published in the United
States by Copeland and Day of Boston. The binding of the
volume 1893–1894 resembles that of the *Century Guild Hobby
Horse*, printed on the invariable blue-grey Ingres paper. A
knight in left profile carries a quiver and a swirling banner
which occupies the upper portion of the design (a motif
related to Horne's designs for *Diversi Colores* and Image's
Poems and Carols). Not surprisingly the knight is mounted on
a Hobby Horse, beneath whose decorative caparison his
spurred feet are clearly visible. The cloth bears the device of a
blindfolded Eros, with the motto "Amore Vincit Omnia" repeated in initials. Horne may have been aware of the tradition
of blind Amor as sensual love, but the winged youth is actually
shooting his arrows in the air. The general shape of the design
is of a rectangle within a rectangle, aligned to the rectangular
preference in book design of Horne's associates in the Century
Guild. The ornaments were also designed by Horne, and the
general impression of the new series is quiet and austere, in
part due to a more disciplined management of type. The
words "Century Guild" were dropped from the title. The magazine was now financially on its own. Not only had the partnership between Horne and Mackmurdo been dissolved, but the
Guild itself had by this time petered out.

The new series suggests a return to the antiquarian basis
of the 1890 and 1891 volumes, reflecting Horne's intensifying
interest in art history. From the fantasia of Adam Legendre,

Horne moves to active work in archives, as in his papers on Inigo Jones and Balthazar Gerbier. Predictably, Horne prefers Jones above Wren, who was tainted with the Baroque; he attends to the machinery of Jones's masques, utilizing the Chatsworth drawings. Gerbier's obscure and varied career, as secret diplomat and agent for King Charles's art collection, clearly fascinates Horne. In addition, A. J. Hipkins discussed the musical instruments of the angels in early Italian painting in the National Gallery; Louis Dyer examined Image's designs for Greek types (based on Image's own notes), confessedly an elaboration of Pollard's views and prescriptively using tenth-century manuscript examples. Arnold Dolmetsch followed with a piece on a consort of viols, the viola d'amore, then lyra–viol and the viola da gamba.

Only three issues of the *Hobby Horse* appeared and no announcement was printed about its suspension. Perhaps Horne's interest in archive work proved decisive, or perhaps the break between Lane and Mathews which occurred in 1894 played some part. In April 1894, the first number of the *Yellow Book* appeared and this may be somewhat remotely considered as the successor of the *Hobby Horse*, though a purely commercial rather than a partly private venture.

Horne's own contributions to the *Century Guild Hobby Horse* have so far been viewed in the context and rhythm of each issue rather than for their own sake. The more important articles, though, demand fuller attention—particularly the preface contributed to the issue of January 1889, which so kindled the disapproval of both Galton and Johnson. This is in the nature of a radical credo—exhibiting allegiance to various (and to some degree opposing) masters (Ruskin, Morris, Arnold, Pater), not merely because Horne himself had learned from each, but also because he wished to reconcile the views of others involved in the magazine's direction.

First, the preface fulfills Horne's prescription that tendencies not individuals should be attacked, and if individuals are alluded to, it should be in general terms, not for their particular sins but for their broad ideological submission. The preface attempts a positive approach, though opening with an oblique attack on current orthodoxies, in particular the stress on the duty that art owed to morality, which Horne traces to the Puritan reaction to the Carolean ideal of "manners and beauty." He suggests that it is these qualities rather than morality that art should now be embodying: "At any one moment in the life of a nation the need of morality may seem to be paramount; but a study of its continued history will show that it has other needs of equal importance." And turning to the chief feature of contemporary art, its commercialization, not unconnected with English puritanism, Horne argues that commercialized art will soon cease to be art in any real sense: "The clay in the brick-field, the wool in the loom, the colour upon the canvas, suddenly become sensitive as the human touch itself, laying bare with appalling certainty, in what spirit the workmen have used them." After his bracing moment of Ruskin and Morris, Horne argues that far from commerce agrandising empires, it destroys both empires and arts. He then turns with some abruptness to the other principal enemy of contemporary art: French art and literature.

True, this enemy is not governed by commercial interests, nor can it be argued that its practitioners take no pleasure in their work. But that work is not truly artistic, for it is conceived in the spirit of science. The allusion here is clearly to Impressionism and Naturalism. Horne's polemic is rendered formulaically: Art submits things to the mind; science submits the mind to things. Zola analyzes social disease but confessedly leaves the remedy to the legislator. The artist, according to him, is essentially disinterested. Against this Horne urges that "In the successive histories of Greece, Rome, medieval Europe, and of more recent times, how differing Art has been both in regard to its ideals and temper, how various in its methods of thought and work, and yet only quality constantly recurs, the endeavour after *fine* interest." We then proceed to Arnold with the onset of "inner culture" representing "the refining away of all that hinders in us the spiritual faculty," and from there to a definition of style: "the delicate balance between the matter to be expressed and the manner of expressing it," of which Virgil remains the palmary example.

Horne then turns to his favourite theme: the centrality of architecture, both metaphorically and actually. "It is not until we come to the study of Architecture," he says, "that the conditions of the highest Art are unmistakably and irrefutably brought before us." The greatest qualities of Art, we are told, are the consequences of much discipline, and Horne alludes to, but does not quote, the first sentence of Vitruvius's *Ten Books of Architecture*: "The architect should be equipped with knowledge of many branches of study and varied kinds of learning, for it is by his judgement that all work done by the other arts is put to the test." Architecture is queen of the arts (which can hardly have pleased those ambitious *littérateurs*, Galton and Johnson). Indeed architecture is the total art and by analogy the architect is the total artist. As the modulator of our environment, his work remains of supreme civic importance.

Judgment consists—it is the essence of Horne's criticism of any of the arts—in knowledge of how to relate parts to the whole, so ensuring fitness, harmony, proportion, and symmetry. The final success of sculpture and the decorative arts is impossible without the architectural sense. And as Horne's early note on the architectural principle in Bach's Fugues and Milton's *Sampson Agonistes* indicates, he invariably applies this species of "form criticism" to past as well as to contemporary works of art, whether discussing the new reredos at St.

Paul's, pointing out the human proportions and the relationship of part to part of the cathedral's west front, or in con-
trasting St. Mary-Le-Strand with the superficially imposing but
actually confused new erections in Northumberland Avenue;
or, again, as in this preface, where he condemns a new statue
of General Gordon. The point is unmistakable: artists should
master the more difficult sense of mass in architecture before
turning to the other arts.

By a somewhat sharp transition, Horne proceeds to
define the title of the magazine and its mode of polemic. There
can be no compromise "in the matter of the fundamental
immutable principles of Art, but in the manner of their individual expression, what we playfully call 'men's hobbies,' those
have their place." Then by yet another rapid transition, we
pass to the familiar complaint that while it is usual to place the
fine arts in relation, particularly in architectural relation, to one
another, what of the decorative, or minor architectural arts? At
this point, intoning disconcertingly, Pater appears:

> In charming us into activity, they [the arts] are able to cheat us of the
> weariness, the *ennui* of life; and in their unbounded capacity to take
> to themselves our energies, they lessen the restlessness of life. Who,
> then, would not endeavour to labour to this end, looking forward to
> no Utopia, but to that day when Art, neither severed nor discarded,
> shall steadily burn as with one flame, and assuredly be counted
> among the number of the divine consolatories.[26]

Yet this apocalypse of total art is not the clausulum; rather the
preface closes gloomily and elliptically with the remark that
partial success only can be expected owing to the nature of the
age.

It remains ironic that Horne was not altogether able to
embody his own prescriptions as to symmetry in this piece. If
the transitions are abrupt, the prose is alternately crabbed and

vatically vague. Horne had little of Image's limpid gift for exposition of general ideas.

About the other articles not touched on, it is possible to be more summary. The three segments of the essay on James Gibbs's life and public works (January, April and July, 1889) are notable for an early use of archive material at the Soane Museum and elsewhere. It is unfortunate, according to Horne, that as to the second of Gibbs's two really fine buildings, the Radcliffe Camera, the germ of the design and the notion of the square around it, are now given to Nicholas Hawksmoor, an architect of whom Horne has little good to say.

What is intriguing about the article on the new reredos at St. Paul's is the question of Horne's attitude to Bernini and the Baroque. Gibbs's talent, we are told, had been nurtured by contact with Bernini's principles of art through Carlo Fontana, by contact, so Horne expresses it, with the best of late Renaissance art. But elsewhere Horne's view is that the true heirs of Renaissance architecture are English, not Italian: Jones and Wren. Nevertheless Horne praises the skillful placing of the "colossal statues" which stand above the bases of the campanili, especially the manner in which we think of them as "figures only a little above the life." "We may see in it," he continues, a little defensively perhaps, the "'ultima manus' or if we are people entirely of this country, as a mere trick." Though Horne's first visit to Italy lay a year ahead, some obscure conversion has already occurred.

It is true that these figures, in Horne's view, are not the consequence of a facile wrenching of perspective. But why do they impress the eye with a "visionary grandeur"? Perhaps because the effect is not mere illusionism, but grows out of Wren's deliberate use of scale in the whole of the West front. The deception of the eye is organically related to its ambience. Horne measures by the imagined figure of a man standing in relation to the façade. But the assertion might have been more convincing if Horne had distinguished Wren's effect at St. Paul's with those figures scenographically poised over the colonnade of St. Peter's in Rome. Bernini, besides subordinating the arts to architecture—his baldichino at St. Peter's would have also made a relevant comparison—had an anthropomorphic conception of the art of building. But perhaps Horne approved of him as a small scale sculptor and painter. At all events he seems to have sufficiently mellowed towards the great seicento artist in later years, for in the catalogue of the Museo Horne, No. 117, there appears Bernini's *Angels in Glory*, an unfinished model in terracotta.

In October 1887 a remarkable woodcut by Selwyn Image entitled *Hiems* figured in an issue of the *Century Guild Hobby Horse*. It consisted of a hooded barefoot figure extending her hands over a fire, whose writhing flames are reminiscent of Art Nouveau. A large tree, whose roots extend across the bottom of the design, frame the figure on left, and two additional trees behind establish a woodland setting. Two birds who nestle in branches above and in the foreground render the negative white shapes of flowers silhouetted against the dark tones of tree bark. This distinctly unusual, though not altogether untraditional, use of woodcut was sharply attacked in the *Pall Mall Gazette* of 17 October 1887.

Horne offered a response to this attack in the following issue of his magazine, a piece entitled "Some Remarks on the Principles of Wood-Cutting." A defensive stress is laid upon abstract autonomy of line and mass and on the principle of fidelity to material. The argument, in fact, is as forward-looking as Image's *Hiems* itself. Rejecting a naturalistic mode of representation, Horne suggests that the woodcutter can take advantage of the medium's very limitations. The main fault, so he sees it, of contemporary woodcutting lies in imitating wash drawing: "Indeed, anything is aimed at but a delight in the precious quality [woodcutting] possesses, the vigour of the black and white."[27] Two main approaches to woodcutting are distinguished: the draughtsman's, of which a typical example is Poliphilo's *Hypernorotomachia* and the preferred method; the engraver's, the manner of Blake and Thomas Bewick, where no division exists between artist and engraver.

A letter to Fairfax Murray of 25 October 1891 provides something of a *terminus ab quo* for Horne's serious interest in Italian archive work.[28] In that letter, he speaks of entering into a series of biographies illustrating the history of art in England from 1500 to 1750; this would be done with the help of his friend Lionel Cust (later the Surveyor of the King's Pictures). The first volume was to have included the life of Torrigiano, the sculptor who worked for Henry VIII, and Horne asks Murray to look at three contracts and a letter in the Florentine archives which Milanesi mentions in the notes to his edition of Vasari.

Under the pseudonym of Lyell Aubryson, Horne published some delicate pastiche of seventeenth-century archive material, "The Papers of Adam Legendre," in the 1890 and 1891 volumes of the *Century Guild Hobby Horse*. It represents a middleground between the Paterian "Imaginary Portrait" and the patient archival evidence that was to support Horne's great book on Botticelli. Like Pater's *Imaginary Portraits*, Legendre's letters become mythicized autobiography, relating to Horne's farewell to the muse of poetry. Legendre is acting at court an antic role in D'Avenant's masque *Salmacida Spolia* when he hears the news of his beloved's death:

> The while these things were proceeding to their Issue, came one Booted and Spurr'd, forcing his way, with much ado, through that Crowd of Gallants, and whispering to my Ear, that she was suddenly departed out of this World, who was the End and Reason of my Continuance therein. And that same instant, was I nam'd for my Entry; and so constrain'd, as I was, in a clownish Habit of the fantastical Shape, which could be devis'd to enact the Drolleries of my Part, and with a thousand apish Mows conceal my true Countenance; until such

Time as a Shift in the Scene should discover the King, under the
character of Philogenes, the healing Wisdom of his People. In the
confusion of that moment, stealing away unperceiv'd, and allowing
myself scarce time enough for a change of Habit, I call'd for a Horse
and rode Night and Day until I had reacht Gataker.[29]

In later years we read Adam Legendre becomes an enigmatic
recluse, "a cloistered man . . . too Saturnine even for my
kindest friend," as he himself observes, the description fore-
shadowing Horne's later phase.[30]

That the years 1890 and 1891 were crucial in Horne's
movement from Pre-Raphaelite "imagination" can be signifi-
cantly shown in the field of Medieval and Renaissance music
and instruments. Where Rossetti's "titherns and citoles" are
mere stunning words or subordinate elements in a painting,
Horne's interest, fortuitously perhaps, was practically directed.

Horne and Arnold Dolmetsch met first in June 1890 when
Horne attended a pupil's concert given by Dolmetsch at the
Portman Rooms. Horne wrote congratulating Dolmetsch on
the performance and enclosed a copy of the *Century Guild
Hobby Horse*. Dolmetsch was delighted and by return thanked
Horne for his support, promising to call within a few days. It
marked the beginning of a friendship which, despite one
major disagreement, was to last till Horne's death. The precise
cause of that disagreement we do not know, but the gap in the
correspondence between the two men extends from 1899 to
1914. For much of this period, though, Dolmetsch was in the
United States, while Horne was mainly in Italy. Dolmetsch
certainly regretted the break; he had an acute respect for
Horne and remained always grateful for Horne's constant
assistance. It was Horne who organized Dolmetsch's first
concert at the Fitzroy Settlement on 19 December 1891, and it
was Horne who published Dolmetsch's article on the Consort
Viols in the *Hobby Horse* (1893). This article and the other
concerts that followed during the decade without doubt

established Dolmetsch's reputation as the recognised pioneer in the revival of early European music.

Through such concerts, Dolmetsch came into touch with Burne-Jones, who brought Morris to hear Dolmetsch for the first time. Morris it appears felt an immediate affinity with this such as he had never experienced with any other music and was soon on friendly terms with Dolmetsch. It was Morris who was responsible for Dolmetsch being made a member of the Art Worker's Guild, probably in 1894, while in 1896 he encouraged Dolmetsch to make his first harpsichord for the Arts and Crafts Exhibition of 1896. This was the famous "green" harpsichord, decorated by Horne, Helen Combe and Selwyn Image.[31] That it should be Morris and not Horne who actively encouraged the re-creation of this instrument is significant. Through association with Mackmurdo and with Morris himself, Horne must have controlled the principle on which Morris worked: the mastery of dead skills by reconstruction from objects and from old manuals. Horne, however, despite his assistance in decorating the "green" harpsichord, was probably less concerned now with re-creation than with the original object *tout court.*

In 1896 and 1897, Horne influenced Dr. Ludwig Mond (later Chairman of I.C.I.) to sponsor the tour of Italy of Dolmetsch and his family "consort." There are frequent references also in Dolmetsch's letters to manuscripts in the museums of Florence and Bologna which Horne had copied and sent to him. The surviving letters between the two men reveal a sharp contrast of personalities. Dolmetsch trusts Horne with many personal confidences, speaking with an engaging frankness of his wife's health, of his divorce problems, of quarrels with critics and of recurrent financial difficulties. Dolmetsch's fluctuating moods are all vividly expressed. The comparatively few letters that survive from Horne to Dolmetsch betray little of the writer's emotions. Kindly and precise, they attend firmly to the matter in hand. Dolmetsch may well have sensed some answering quality in Horne which remains absent from his letters. The range of his letters was probably limited by the fact that Dolmetsch belonged neither to literary Bohemia nor to the world of art historians and collectors out of which gossip could be accomplished. But Horne may well have glimpsed a younger, more naïve and idealistic self mirrored in Dolmetsch, along with other attributes prized and now lost. The nature of the affinity between the two men is at all events not discoverable in the record.

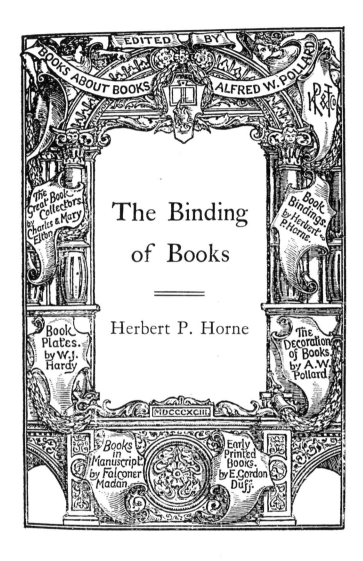

The following text appears within the title-page design:

EDITED BY

BOOKS ABOUT BOOKS

ALFRED W. POLLARD

The Binding
of Books

Herbert P. Horne

The Great Book-Collectors by Charles & Mary Elton

Book Bindings by Herbert P. Horne

Book Plates by W.J. Hardy

The Decoration of Books by A.W. Pollard

MDCCCXCIII

Books in Manuscript by Falconer Madan

Early Printed Books by E. Gordon Duff

fig. 6.1 *The Binding of Books*, title-page design

CHAPTER 6

The Typographer and Book Design

These were the years also of the Rhymers' Club and of its hero Verlaine's visit in 1893 to London, organized jointly by Horne and Symons. The part that Horne played among the Rhymers in the Club is difficult to determine. Having abandoned poetry, he did not contribute either to the first or the second of the Club's anthologies, but he was certainly prominent in club discussions. His interests, as we have seen, were far wider than most of the Rhymers. He was becoming well known in the world of architects and decorators, and whenever there was any question of a fine building being demolished, badly restored or decorated, Horne was certain to be among those who publicly protested.

In these years, also, he began to write prolifically on a wide variety of topics. The direction of such new interests can be gathered from an article on Venetian Missals published in 1894. Horne's ideal of book-production emerges from the concluding generalisation, and corresponds closely with the ideals of the *Century Guild Hobby Horse*. Remarking that the 1880s and 1890s had witnessed increased attention to book-production in all its aspects, Horne still finds the result unsatisfactory when judged by the standards of the Renaissance. Few books "possess those qualities of repose, and of simple, effective decoration, which distinguish the illustrated books of Florence and Venice, during the great period of the printer's art."[1] This article is important as the first manifestation of Horne's reaction against the movement of taste in the 1890s: it counters Art Nouveau and French influence on literature in its more radical effects.

In *The Binding of Books* (1894), a volume contributed to Alfred W. Pollard's Books About Books series (6.1), Horne disputes the statement—made not surprisingly by a Frenchman—that "La Reliure est un art tout française." His own ideal of repose and severity in binding, as in typography and architecture, Horne finds in the Italy of the sixteenth century. It is particularly the Venetian bindings executed for the great Jean de Servières Grolier, whose energies extended always to "scholarly sympathy and scrupulous taste," that capture Horne's admiration. Above all the Grolier bindings possess an architectonic quality, a quality progressively extinguished in the more technically sophisticated French tradition. Such an architectonic criterion is constant with Horne. He applies it to all forms of art and it is, as we know, the continuous theme of his critical articles in the *Century Guild Hobby Horse*.

Horne's book is dedicated to T. J. Cobden-Sanderson, who has "done for book-binding what Mr. William Morris has done for glass-painting, tapestry-weaving, and other decorative arts."[2] The particular production Horne chose as representative of Cobden-Sanderson's work is a copy of T. J. Wise's facsimile edition of Shelley's *Adonais*. The binding is orange-red morocco and the surface is elaborately powdered with stars and flower-heads. Whatever the distinction of workmanship this design possesses, it certainly diverges from any ideal of severity and repose. Its principle is less architectonic than decorative. Horne's eclecticism challenges his austerity of taste when he comments, "strictures may be passed upon his work" but "he has invented a distinguished manner of his own. . . . In his hands, gilt-tooling has again become a living art."[3]

Horne did not himself practice gilt tooling. The recognition then of Cobden-Sanderson's achievement in binding is faintly grudging. The Cobden-Sanderson *Adonais,* though not in a pronouncedly Art Nouveau mode, employs those stylized flower-forms. The rejection, or at most limited approval, of modern work in the applied arts involved rejection not merely of the practice, but also of the theory behind modern work. That involved "free" illustration, which is personal and subjective, rather than "architectural" in its composition. The notion that the ornament of a binding should emblematize or be in some manner expressive of a book's contents, Horne observes, can be traced back to the Middle Ages; but it is the French who have pursued this principle, though rarely with success, to its logical conclusion:

> At the present day, the notion has been carried to its extreme by some designers, who, affecting the fashion of the Decadents, appear to work in a spirit akin to that of Arthur Rimbaud's sonnet, which finds, in colours, the definite sensations of language.[4]

Rimbaud's sonnet on the vowels, whether or not the poet was in fact describing the coloured letters of a child's reading primer, as some have suggested, is, like Baudelaire's sonnet "Correspondences," one of the early crystallisations of *symboliste* doctrine. The implications of Horne's comments amount to a rejection of total art in the making of a book, a rejection not merely, say, of Charles Ricketts and Lucien Pisarro, the Vale and the Eragny Presses, but of Blake himself.

Horne and Image clearly owe more to the Arts and Crafts tradition than to Mackmurdo's proto-art book design. Horne's earliest design for his collection of poems *Diversi Colores*

(1891) is barely successful (6.2). The blue-grey paper of the cover derives from the brown paper covers of Whistler's designs for his own books. The design of the title-page is over-weighted and the lettering, as observed before, is split phonetically, though arbitrarily in the imprint. The model here is probably Image's cover design for *Primavera* (1890), an anthology of verses by four young Oxford poets, Laurence Binyon, Stephen Phillips, A. S. Cripps, and Manmohan Ghose. The motif Image settled on was a long-stemmed branch with free formalized flower buds. The title itself is broken up by the foliage. Morris's cover design for *Love is Enough* (1873), we may remember, furnishes an earlier example. The motif was to be repeated in Image's designs for Elkin Mathews's Shilling Garland series. Horne's design for Image's *Poems and Carols* (1894) is even less successful than *Diversi Colores*. The letter-ing once more splits arbitrarily and non-phonetically (6.3).

Poèms sans rimes by Olivier Georges Destrée (1894) is the first of Horne's achieved designs (6.4). Grey Ingres paper is used for the cover. The title-page, typography and initial letters are all by Horne. A somewhat pictorial woodcut design was printed on hand-made paper. The floral motif interrupts the title, date and imprint, and actually bisects in the apostro-phe of "L'Auter." Possibly there was some French influence, not inappropriately, for Destrée was a Walloon. The layout of the page here is an example of the positive use of white space.

The design of Lionel Johnson's *Poems* (1895) is finely austere, answering the persona presented by Johnson in that volume (6.5). The centre of the title-page is occupied by a rubricated version of a rectangular fifteenth-century woodcut representing William of Wykeham, founder of St. Mary's College at Winchester, while Johnson in his dedication describes himself as a Wykehamist come of Wykehamists. The first poem has for its subject the school, and the note of the poems is hieratic, Latin Catholic, medieval. In the list of con-

tents, the page numbers of individual poems immediately
follow the titles (6.6), a practice now widespread, but one
which Horne appears to have initiated with his design for
Symons's *Silhouettes* of 1892. In the large paper presentation
copy of that volume, Horne wrote "The text of this book was
already in type when Symons asked me to look to the printing
of it. Except for designing the title, I only managed the pages,
heading, etc. and composed the 'contents.'"

In 1895 also, Horne designed the cover, title-page and
contents page for Frank Harris's *Elder Conklin and Other
Stories* (6.7, 6.8). Like the Johnson *Poems* this was commissioned by a commercial publisher. The cover design includes
wittily in Ricketts's manner four of the short story titles
arranged according to visual harmony and concluded by an
elaborate "&c." The printing, as in all of Horne's earlier
designs, was accomplished by the Chiswick Press. Their colophon, rubricated on the final page of Johnson's text (6.8), is
now placed at the centre of the title-page. The typical severity
and repose of this title-page are somewhat offset by stylized
leaves, prolonging the shorter lines of the title.

The designs of Horne's middle period include the urn on
the title-page of *The Golden Urn,* a private magazine edited by
Bernard Berenson and Logan Pearsall Smith and published at
Fiesole between 1897 and 1898. Horne may also have had a
hand in the layout. In 1903 there followed an edition of Sir
Henry Wotton's *The Elements of Architecture,* commissioned
by Longman's Green (6.9). The cover once more was of blue-
grey Ingres paper, with an affixed label on the spine. Horne
designed the title-page, with three stylized flowers rubricated,
the ornaments including the urn already furnished for
Berenson's periodical, and initials rubricated within a stylized
circular stem. In 1902, moreover, Horne had furnished the
cover design for the *Burlington Magazine,* in whose foundation he had assisted, which survived for more than thirty years.

In 1909 the prospectus of the Riccardi Press Book was printed in the Riccardi type designed by Horne and based, so the prospectus tells us, on the larger of the two faces used in the famous first edition of Horace printed in Florence in 1492 by Antonio Misconsino. In the *Anthanaeum* of November 1909, however, Horne demurred to the description, suggesting that it was better termed "an attempt to produce a modern equivalent of the Misconsino fount." Of the Riccardi, and the two other types Horne at this time designed—the Montallegro and the Florence (6.10)—Robert Steele in his *The Revival of Printing* (1912) observes that all three "show a continuous tendency to a richer line, and I may be permitted to say here that the latter is, to my mind, as nearly perfect a letter in the style [Horne] aims at as can be imagined."[5] *The Revival of Printing*, it may also be observed, was printed in Riccardi for the Riccardi Press.

Marius the Epicurean (1913), also from the Riccardi Press and using Riccardi type, was a tribute to an old master. The border on the title-page probably relates to late eighteenth-century woodcuts, while the letter forms attempt to follow the spiral of Renaissance inscriptional lettering (6.11). The rectangular shape is familiarly Century Guild but without rubrication, while the close-knit arrangement of text pages is in keeping with the preferences of designers of the private press movement for a strongly textured page, coupled with wide margins (6.12). The source here is Whistler's arrangement in his various volumes, though Whistler has rather disconcertingly arranged his footnotes flanking the text on both sides. A similar arrangement can be found in the Wotton volume, but here the seventeenth-century original is responsible.

Horne was active also in the design of book plates (6.13), and three examples of his work are given in the *Studio* of 1893.[6] The first is a woodblock: the initial "H" set among leaves in Kelmscottian mode. Of the other two designs, that for Fred

DIVERSI COLORES

M·DCC C·XC·I

London Published by the Author at the Chiswick Press.

fig. 6.2 *Diversi Colores*, title-page design

POEMS
& CAROLS

M·DCCC ·XC · IV

London·
by·Elkin·
Vigo·Street·w

Published
Mathews

fig. 6.3 *Poems and Carols,* title-page design

P O È M E S
S A N S
R I M E S

1 8 9 4

LONDRES IMPRIMÉ
POVR L' AVTEVR

fig. 6.4 *Poèms sans rimes*, title-page design

P·O·E·M·S
BY · LIONEL
JOHNSON

1 8 9 5

LONDON · ELKIN MATHEWS
BOSTON · COPELAND & DAY

fig. 6.5 *Poems*, title-page design

CONTENTS.

ix

fig. 6.6 *Poems*, contents page design

ELDER CONKLIN AND OTHER STORIES BY FRANK HARRIS

LONDON
W. HEINEMANN
M·DCCC·XC·V

fig. 6.7 *Elder Conklin and Other Stories*, title-page design

CONTENTS.

fig. 6.8 *Elder Conklin and Other Stories,* contents page design
Chiswick Press colophon design

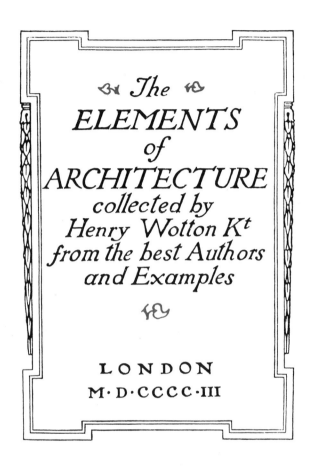

&⟨ *The* ⟩&

ELEMENTS
of
ARCHITECTURE
collected by
Henry Wotton K^t
from the best Authors
and Examples

&

L O N D O N
M·D·CCCC·III

fig. 6.9 *The Elements of Architecture,* title-page design

And if you set him beneath as good a man as him
self at the table: that is against his honour. If you
do not visite him at home at his house: then you
knowe not your dutie. Theis maner of fashions and
behaviours, bring men to such scorne and disdaine
of their doings: that there is no man, almost, can
abide to beholde them : for they love them selves
to farre beyonde measure, and busie them selves
so much in that, that they finde litle leisure to

La lungheza di decta chiesa insulata e braccia du-
cento sexanta: la quale di fuori e tucta di uarii marmi
incrustata, con statue di marmo et porphiri molto
adornata per mano di nobili sculptori; maxime di
Donato ui e il gigante primo, dalla porta della As-
sumptione marmorea per mano di Iohanni Banchi,
sopra la Annuntiata di musiuo per mano di Domenico
Grillandaro. Nella facciata dinanzi e uno euangelista
a sedere et una statua di uno che si piegha, et in sul
cantone uno uecchio, tucte per mano di Donato. Ma
a dirti la uerita, decta facciata, la quale Lorenzo de'

and it is no exaggeration to say that in no printed
book between the closing years of the fifteenth
century and those of the nineteenth was any attempt made to obtain them all, though the tra-
ditions of good craftsmanship ensured that some
of them were preserved in many cases. The
fifteenth-century book was avowedly an imita-
tion of a fine manuscript; its type was a copy
of the current writing hand, the arrangement of
its page was that of a manuscript, its spacing

fig. 6.10 Montallegro, Florence, Riccardi
Horne's designs

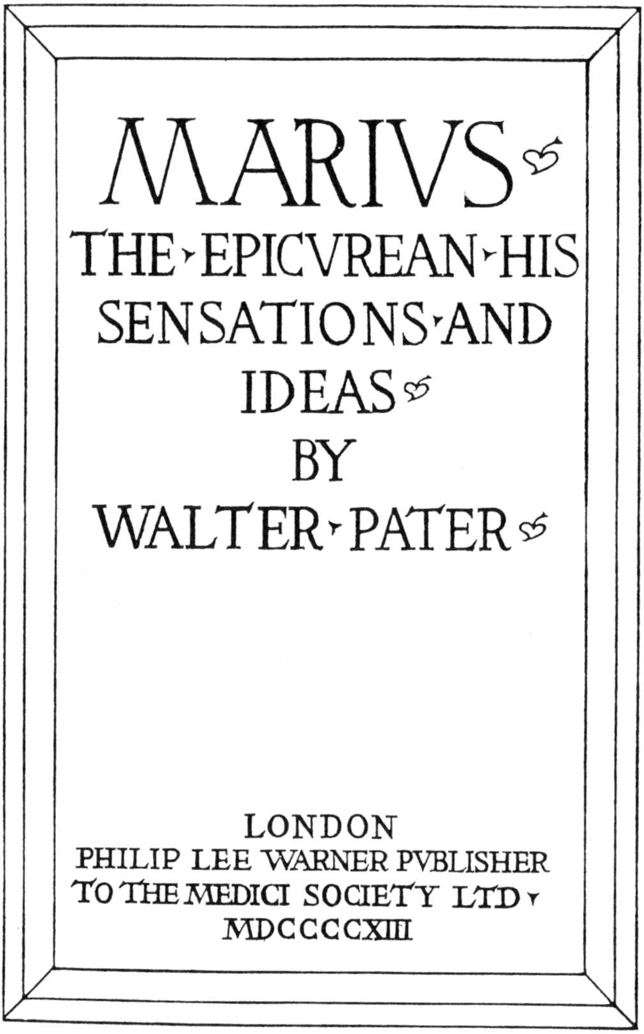

MARIVS ✿
THE·EPICVREAN·HIS
SENSATIONS·AND
IDEAS ✿
BY
WALTER·PATER ✿

LONDON
PHILIP LEE WARNER PVBLISHER
TO THE MEDICI SOCIETY LTD ·
MDCCCCXIII

fig. 6.11 *Marius the Epicurean*, title-page design

PART THE FIRST

CHAPTER I. 'THE RELIGION OF NUMA'

AS, in the triumph of Christianity, the old religion lingered latest in the country, and died out at last as but paganism – the religion of the villagers, before the advance of the Christian Church; so, in an earlier century, it was in places remote from town-life that the older and purer forms of paganism itself had survived the longest. While, in Rome, new religions had arisen with bewildering complexity around the dying old one, the earlier and simpler patriarchal religion, 'the religion of Numa,' as people loved to fancy, lingered on with little change amid the pastoral life, out of the habits and sentiment of which so much of it had grown. Glimpses of such a survival we may catch below the merely artificial attitudes of Latin pastoral poetry; in Tibullus especially, who has preserved for us many poetic details of old Roman religious usage.

At mihi contingat patrios celebrare Penates,
Reddereque antiquo menstrua thura Lari:

– he prays, with unaffected seriousness. Something liturgical, with repetitions of a consecrated form of words, is traceable in one of his elegies, as part of the order of a birthday sacrifice. The hearth, from a spark of which, as one form of old legend related, the child Romulus had been miraculously born, was still indeed an altar; and the worthiest sacrifice to the gods the perfect physical sanity of the young men and women, which the scrupulous ways of that religion of the hearth had tended to maintain. A religion of usages and sentiment rather than of facts and belief, and attached to very definite things and places – the oak of immemorial age, the rock on the heath fashioned by weather as if by some dim human art, the shadowy grove of ilex, passing into which one exclaimed involuntarily, in consecrated phrase, Deity is in this place! 'Numen Inest!' – it was in natural harmony with the temper of a quiet people amid the spectacle of rural life, like that

3

fig. 6.12 *Marius the Epicurean*, text design
Riccardi typeface

fig. 6.13 Book plates: Horne's 'H'
Constitution Club, Fred Trehawk Davies

Trehawk Davies consists in a rondel made up of three hawks facing outward set against a series of diminishing circles, perching on stems that curve into the client's initials. This is an attractive offsetting. The Constitutional Club design is more formalised: a crown surmounting a crossed sword and cane reversed with a knob, capitalised "c" and the same letter reversed, the whole, surrounded by rose and thistle foliage. Unlike Anning Bell's bookplates featured also in the same issue of the *Studio*, Horne's are not merely decorative and picturesque, with visual puns and precise content; they acquire some emblematic force. This appears to run counter to Horne's criteria for the book, but tradition sanctioned such features for what was a highly personal sign. Among Horne's correspondence with his friend Randall Davies, moreover, is a design and interesting comment on how the designer arrived at his results.

Horne also made designs for several gravestones. One is in Gli Allori, an attractive cemetery just southwest of Florence. The plain rectangle with lettering in Renaissance script commemorates his mother Hannah Louisa Horne, who died in 1903. This design accords with Horne's later ideals. A letter of 29 May 1895 from a New College contemporary of Lionel Johnson, the Rev. William Busby, a contributor to the *Century Guild Hobby Horse* (at the time curate of St. Faith's, Norwich), records that Horne had designed a cross for the grave of his client's son. Busby invites Horne to make a drawing for his aunt, Antonia Whately: "in a circle like the other, and in the same Lombard lettering."

The architectonic principle is once more invoked in an article on "The Strand Improvements."[7] Here, Horne applies an aesthetic based on chiaroscuro in painting to architecture and ultimately to complexes and town-planning. The aberrations of nineteenth-century London architecture can be equally measured against the ideals of the High Renaissance, but judgment of some of Michelangelo's masterpieces demands very delicate criteria. At once the consummation and for the purist perhaps the betrayer of the Renaissance *symmetria magna*, Michelangelo in such a work as the ante-room of the Laurenziana Library might seem to an orthodox admirer of Renaissance serenity to have committed an act of heroic bad taste. Horne, reviewing Symonds's work on the master, recognises, as he does in St. Paul's though without altogether approving, the structural paradoxes of the ante-room. We must not of course assume that Michelangelo is in any sense incompetent. Horne adduces typically the grammatical errors in Michelangelo's poetry as in no way proving him to be a poetaster:

> The boldness of the staircase, with its strange triple ascent to the half-pace; the extraordinary subtlety of the order which rises above it, the reticence of the superior order, here scarcely begun, there almost completed, the rough timbered roof hastily thrown across the walls, as if merely intended to keep out the weather, forcibly arrest the attention, like one of the unfinished figures in the neighboring sacristy . . . The strong, almost violent forms which compose the staircase, the oval steps, the ellipse on the half-pace, justify the use of the consoles, placed beneath the recessed columns, which are ranged about the walls; and the gradual transition from the boldness of these curves to the reticence of the upper order, seems to lend the whole work a kind of unity. I say that this appears to be so; for the effect intended by the whole work, when finished, cannot be concluded from this fragment.[8]

Horne, unlike Burckhardt, at least recognises Michelangelo's seriousness and this is admirable close criticism of the disturbing interior of the ante-room. To stress the incompleteness of the work is perhaps too facile an escape from the spectatorial uneasiness, an uneasiness which—whether or not one accepts Pevsner's categorisation of the Laurenziana as "Mannerist"—is clearly intended by the architect.[9]

The intensified journalism of the years from 1894 on owes something to the collapse of the *Century Guild Hobby Horse* and Horne's release from editorial pressures, not to mention the need for money. As we know, for years the *Century Guild Hobby Horse* had been running not merely at a loss, but on unbusinesslike lines. So did its successor, the *Hobby Horse*. Horne owed Mackmurdo money, or at least Mackmurdo thought he did. An inaccurate account of the bitterness that flared up between Mackmurdo and Horne and later between Horne and Image is given by Ernest Rhys in his two volumes of reminiscences, *Everyman Remembers* and *Wales England Wed*:

> When I first met him Horne talked of Image with boyish idolatry . . . Years went on, and then, to my dismay, I heard there had been a break between Horne and Image. A marked change came over Horne from the days he first met Oscar Wilde, and I believe his alienation from his old friend may be traced to the years when he fell under that evil spell. The worst Image ever allowed himself to say was, it was Horne's want of loyalty that hurt him most.[10]

Image, in fact, was in the awkward position of mediating between Mackmurdo and Horne, and as Horne seems to have owed Mackmurdo money it is not surprising that Image should have taken Mackmurdo's part.[11] A letter from Image to Mackmurdo of 19 September 1895 pathetically reads: "Can't we settle up and sign and seal this blooming agreement 'twixt you and H without further delay! H will most likely be going away shortly, and the lawyer may get troublesome. . . . I desire peace and quiet for us one and all."[12]

For Horne to have built up his collections on relatively slender resources and to have devoted himself so single-mindedly to the life of the connoisseur involved a certain ruthlessness and detachment. As late as 1900 he writes to

Edgar Jepson, who was at that time occupying Horne's rooms at 4 King's Bench Walk during the winter and spring months:

> Would you kindly make a point of forwarding to me any letters bearing the name of G. D. Freeman, Solicitor, 16 Paul St., Finsbury Square, stamped on the envelope. This worthy person has been sent by Mackmurdo to extort more money out of me, in connection with the Hobby Horse. If you receive any visits, please know nothing except that I am abroad.[13]

Like the *Germ*, the *Century Guild Hobby Horse* died in a context of financial squalor. We do not know enough about its finances or about the nature of the agreement between Mackmurdo and Horne to judge the moral issue. It seems certain that Mackmurdo's attempts to belittle Horne's part in the Century Guild and its magazine stem from their quarrel. Of Image, Horne writes to Jepson on 21 December 1900: "All I have done is like the gentleman in the psalms—to hold my tongue and say nothing. I am very sorry but I do not see what else I could have done under the circumstances."[14] The tone is milder certainly, but it is clear that Horne had rejected his "aesthetic" past and that both of his mentors were too much associated with that past, though he remained friendly with Image.

As early as 1895 in his *Saturday Review* articles, Horne had reacted against the Art Nouveau tendencies of the Guild. On 7 August 1900, reviewing the Exhibition of Art Students' Drawings for the National Competition, he wrote:

> Instead of being encouraged to draw from the life, the students are set to make patterns and invent ornaments in the latest and most meretricious school of decorative design which had its origin in the "Arts and Crafts" Exhibitions, and which has now found a home in Tottenham Court Road.

And of the *Studio* and other contemporary German magazines:

> In emulation of their exemplars, they impart to the forms of all natural
> objects—be they figures or flowers—the convolution of loames and
> entrails. The whole thing is a trick which anyone with a little gift for
> drawing can acquire in a very short time; that no doubt, is one of the
> secrets of its immense popularity. But the invention of ornament,
> even when it is fine ornament, is but a small part of decorative art.[15]

On 14 August, Horne returned to the theme:

> As long ago as the early eighties, a designer little known to the public
> at large, Mr. A. H. Mackmurdo, had invented and fully developed
> what I called "the swirl and a blob" manner of pattern-making. He, if I
> mistake not, was its real originator; though I believe he derived some
> of his ideas from Mr. Gilbert, the sculptor. And not only did he then
> design wallpapers and cretonnes, but furniture, and even houses, in a
> way that would allow them to pass today with the newest production
> of the school. From Mr. Mackmurdo, Mr. C. F. A. Voysey derived
> bodily all his ideas of architecture and decoration.[16]

From 1894 on, then, Horne wrote regularly for the *Saturday Review*, and we can trace from such reviews and articles the change in his interests. The subjects treated include "Bach and the Harpsichord" (15 December 1894), "The Sforza Book of Hours" (Supplement, 15 December 1894), and "Botticelli and Savonarola" (13 August 1898).

Towards the turn of the century, Horne was contributing to the *Review of the Week* and as "H" he was writing weekly "Art Notes" for the *Morning Leader*, while still contributing to the *Saturday Review* and the *Star*.[17]

ALESSANDRO FILIPEPI
COMMONLY CALLED
SANDRO BOTTICELLI
PAINTER OF
FLORENCE

◀ BY ▶
HERBERT P. HORNE

LONDON
GEORGE BELL & SONS
M·D·CCCCVIII

fig. 7.1 *Alessandro Filipepi*, title-page design

CHAPTER 7

The Art Historian:
Italy and Botticelli

From the years 1894–1895 on, Horne was to spend much
time in Italy. When in London, he utilized his mother's house
at 14 Cheyne Walk, though he kept his rooms for a few years
at 4 Kings Bench Walk (where he designed a fireplace). In
Florence, his life during the 1890s sounds lively enough:

> The coals of love are coals of fire which have an exceeding vehement
> flame; and (tho' the prophet sayeth not) are apt to illuminate divers
> things diversely . . . you know that Bottani and the altar piece (a so-
> called Botticelli) once in the church of St. Maggiore, occupy a con-
> siderable part of my research here. But how different a light has the
> flame of love cast upon all that. How differently, when sated with the
> beauties of Marcellina, I look askance from her window in the Borgo
> degli Albiggi, Numero—(But why should I tell you that). Secondo
> Piano, upon the ruined portico of S. Maggiore. How differently, and
> how nearly does Bottani occur to one—to say nothing of Botti-
> celli—no more, therefore, with your Venetian nights in Florence.
> Enough that Marcellina confesses in me to have found the true "fuoco
> d'amore," and that we are immensely pleased with one another. Why
> should I explain to you that Marcellina is like a madonna of Botticelli,
> only the healthy creature, with none of the Botticellian morbid senti-
> ments about her; none of the maladies of the soul, in short, not one

damned virginal thing in her whole self—you would but smile at me
. . . Find me in your filthy Piccadilly, the girl who knows not what
whisky is; whose aphrodisiac is a cup of hot milk; who has a charming apartment; who would not regard you with more approbation, if
you gave her a fiver, than when you gave her a Lire 20 note! Who
meets you under the shadow of a Donatello or a Michaelangelo: who
is mistress of every Italian sophistry that even *you* could desire. . . . In
brief sir, I wish you Florentine nights in London! . . . Servitore . . .
Herbert P. Horne.[1]

This attempt to make a Restoration Comedy urban-
pastoral out of his Florentine life is not very secure. Marcellina,
successor to the English Violet Percival and Muriel Broadbent,
left him to marry a wealthy *avvocato*. This, he recalls with a
humorous self-pity, is the usual fate of his mistresses.

Marcellina was succeeded by Bianca, with whom Horne
passed a vacation in 1903 at Carcassone. She certainly
enlivened the Florentine scene:

Bianca is in great form here. She has just finished a very smart new
dress . . . and has been sailing about in it to-day, to the admiration of
the town, who has dubbed her "La Misteriosa Francescina." She is
making a collection of the astonishing things which men in the street
say to her, to her vast disgust. They are too slangy to transcribe and
too lewd to translate. "Che bel culo" is one of the more harmless.[2]

Muriel Broadbent had become mysteriously transformed
into Phyllis Hacon, wife of Ricketts's partner in the Vale Press,
and was now a widow, her husband having died in 1910.
Randall Davies met her and described her to Horne as
"buxom." Hearing of Horne's serious ill health she wrote to
him from Dornoch: "I rarely go to London now, my interests
are all here in the North, and lately I have taken up work
among the girls at the Herring Fishing in the Shetlands. I fancy
I can see you smile at the idea—all the same—I am very keen
in the work and am very happy over it." And referring ever so
obliquely to the days of the 1890s: "I was in Edinburgh last

week and on Sunday saw Fr. John Gray. He is very much beloved in Edinburgh and leads a splendid life and does heaps of work. I should so like to hear from you. I wonder whether you remember me."[3]

Laurence Binyon, poet and art critic, was another correspondent of the Florence years. Horne's letters of 17 March and 11 April 1898 to Binyon are of particular interest as indications of how penetrating and pure was Horne's taste. Binyon had invited him to take part in a forthcoming Portfolio series which was to appear under the auspices of the Unicorn Press. To Binyon's suggestion of the Della Robbias, Horne replied:

> Della Robbia is a host of persons, and in general has been admirably written about by Pater. . . . Why not discover somebody? That would be a good "lead off" for your series. Neither Piero della Francesca nor Jacopo Pontormo has ever yet been discovered in a popular sense. I want to do something on Pier Francheschi. . . . Only don't give away my plans for Pontormo.[4]

These two artists roused special critical attention for the second quarter of the twentieth century, though Burne-Jones and Symonds, for example, were expressing high admiration for Piero as early as the 1870s. Binyon then suggested Pisanello, whom Horne approved in his April letter, but added

> let me discover for you Agostino di Duccio, the carver of those beautiful reliefs in the "tempio" at Rimini . . . they are just the kind of decorative art which appeals to English people; and no one has yet written about him . . . one could legitimately indulge in all sorts of pretty writing, which would be out of place and absurd in discussing a really first rate artist like Donatello.[5]

Horne instantly recognised the affinity of Duccio's (or pseudo-Duccio's) wavering low-relief carvings to later Pre-Raphaelitism and Art Nouveau, but his critical rigour constrained him from over-rating these attractive designs.[6]

Though well-known in the Anglo-Florentine world of art historians, virtuosi, and exiles, Horne was to become more of a recluse, particularly after about 1906. It was a closed world, full of delicate gossip and graceful malaise, shadowy jealousies and arcane resentments, the species of quarrels "likely to arise in a small expatriate society not unafflicted with nerves," wrote the editor of Berenson's letters of an exchange between Berenson and Vernon Lee. And William Rothenstein, visiting Florence in the autumn of 1907, responded to the scene by saying "there were armed camps and fierce rivalries in Florence then, as in past times; but the fighting was far less bloody, concerned as it was with attributions rather than with Ducal thrones. Berenson, Horne, Loeser, Vernon Lee, Maude Crutwell, all had their mercenaries—and their artillery."[7]

Of Horne's Florentine career, we can trace a vestige from the letters that Bernard and Mary Berenson exchanged virtually every day of their married life, and also from Mary's journal. As early as 1895, Horne and Berenson had engaged in transactions over paintings. From this period on Horne supplied on commission Ross's Carfax Gallery, but he was never able to attract Berenson's variety of high patronage. In keeping with his costive temperament, Horne's speculation in art works tended perhaps to the frugal and cautious. He was much involved with Roger Fry in dealings, but documentation of these transactions is wanting.

Berenson's first impressions of Horne were not favorable: a trip by bicycle over the Lombard plain is enthusiastically described, but "the one drawback was Horne . . . as it were dropped his mask and betrayed at once an exceeding incapacity for seeing with his own eyes and an excessive eagerness to gather into his notebook all the things he could squeeze out of me about the various galleries we visited."[8] Mary's reaction initially was much more favorable, but wholeheartedly or tactfully we detect her sometimes agreeing with

her husband's sporadic feelings of disquiet and suspicion of
Horne's activities. We find Berenson writing to Ross on 12
January 1908: "Horne is going to England, and as you are I
doubt not an expert oyster-opener, you will get much delecta-
tion."[9] Horne's opacity exercised a fascination over both Ross
and Berenson, unmixed in Ross's case with irritation.

Mary Berenson on 18 August 1908 reports a comment
"doubtless Oscar's, not [Ross's]. He was speaking, as he often
is, of Horne and said his taciturnity was so persistent that no
one else could get in a flash of silence edgeways." And a
genuinely wounded note sounds in a letter of 18 September
1909 from Mary to Berenson: "Horne evidently puts himself in
the right by speaking well of thee and no one can trace (or
believe) his actions against thee." And four days earlier: "I met
Perkins—he 'recognised' a Jacopo del Casentino at Loeser's,
but Horne also guessed it and is going to publish it first."[10]

Whatever their reservations, the Berensons certainly were
helpful to Horne over the Botticelli book. Horne himself was
more ready than might appear to assist the Berensons. A letter
of Mary's in the archives at the Villa I Tatti affords us a glimpse
of Horne turning aside from his absorbed copying of ancient
records to older enthusiasms:

> I went to Houghton's first and asked him if he could get a stone
> doorway from the library. He said Horne had just bought some fine
> ones from Logan [Pearsall Smith] and I went to Horne's . . . Horne was
> there, copying inscriptions. He said he would come up on Sunday
> and look at the room etc. He may be able to suggest something also
> for the awful casa colonica.

Berenson came in the end to recognise Horne's generosity no
less than his unique knowledge of the Italian archives. When
Horne died, Berenson described the event as "a great loss to
our studies and such a waste. Had he lived the usual span of
life he might have done work which would have been of real

value, for he was in his way a living spring."[11] Berenson was a master of qualification. But twenty-two years later in the elaborated version of his *Drawings of the Florentine Painters* Berenson unequivocally acknowledged the permanent value of Horne's study of Botticelli and the generosity Horne consistently showed in furnishing him with archival material. There were clearly sharp temperamental differences between the two men; but their modes of approach to the earlier Renaissance were also radically opposed.

Berenson was no haunter of archives and he had, so he believed, derived a distinct "science" of attribution for his master, Giovanni Morelli, based on the careful comparison of the rendering of minor specialist physical characteristics in figures and, by extension, also aspects of landscape.[12] It was this "system" which allowed Berenson to posit the existence of "Amico di Sandro" in the *Gazette de Beaux Arts* and of "Alunno di Domenicho" in the *Burlington Magazine* (1903): a canon and an unnamed master. "Amico" was later dropped, but the method was not faulted. And Berenson was without the Anglo-Saxon distrust of abstract ideas, of speculation as play-impulse.

Horne, on the other hand, was temperamentally cautious; his attributions were the result of the archival work, published histories, painful comparisons of many details, not ears or left hands. What Berenson described as a "living spring" was Horne's knowledge of the archives. His architectural scholarship and the fruit of these two capacities effected a detailed familiarity with the physical presence of early Renaissance Florence. This enabled Horne to "place" paintings in time and space, to marry vague descriptions in inventories with the length of a particular wall or the height of a particular room. The work of art as a physical no less than as an aesthetic object was central to Horne's understanding: painting as furniture, as programme, propaganda, memorial, ritual. Berenson, whose achievements need no defence, came to see that his and Horne's talents were reciprocal, not antithetical.

At about the time when the Berensons were exchanging their mildly sour letters, Max Beerbohm was in Florence, working on a drawing of Horne under the title of *Celestial Attributions* (7.2). Beerbohm described it to Ross:

> Horne was standing in the foreground, placid and rather heavy, smoking a cigarette. In the sky behind are a Madonna and Child, looking down at Horne with a lively interest expressed in their primitive Siennese faces.
>
> *Virgin:* That's a *very* doubtful Horne.
> *Child:*   M'Yes. It looks to me rather as if it might be an early Berenson . . .
> *Virgin:* Pooh! Nonsense! *Everything* points to its being a particularly late Langton Douglas."[13]

Although mostly involved in the continued study of Botticelli, his sources and school, after the definitive move to Florence (dated variously as the autumn of 1902 or 1904) Horne published other work. From the phase of his most committed interest in English eighteenth-century art dates *An Illustrated Catalogue of engraved portraits and fancy subjects painted by Thomas Gainsborough, published between 1760 and 1820. And by George Romney published between 1770 and 1830 with the variations of the plates* (1891). In 1903 an edition appeared with notes of Vasari's life of Leonardo and the following year a translation of Condivi's life of Michelangelo which for the first time used the type Montallegro, which Horne had designed for the Merrymount Press at Boston, Massachusetts. In 1907 Horne published an *Account of Rome in 1450* based to some degree on a fifteenth-century manuscript.

Horne's first extended article drawing from Florentine archival material, "Uccello's Battle-Piece," was published in

fig. 7.2 *Celestial Attributions*, caricature of Horne
Max Beerbohm

the *Monthly Review* for 1901. The audience was not precisely popular, though certainly not sternly specialist. The argument in this piece hinges on the definition of the event commemorated by Uccello in the National Gallery's official catalogue. It is, says Horne, perfectly inaccurate and "a pedantic piece of absurdity." The National Gallery, indeed, joins the Royal Academy as a polemical topic in Horne's writing. Here he demonstrates by employing his usual types of sources that the subject is not "Carlo Malatetsa, Lord of Rimini, and his nephew Galeazzo taken prisoner by Braccio di Montone" but rather the rout of San Romano when Niccolo da Tolentino and Michelotto da Colognola of the Florentine army defeated the famous *condottiero* Bernardino della Carda. Horne's intention then is to rectify the Gallery's error and to show by what was to become his customary method how it came about.

He started from some plain discrepancies between the National Gallery description of the battle and the actual detail of the painting, proceeds to Varsari's account of Uccello, and then to Vasari's later nineteenth-century editor, the archivist Milanesi who, while furnishing new archival evidence is less energetic in dispelling that *aberglaube* Vasari so agreeably accretes. "Demythologising" of this order is one of Horne's first motives in his art history, but he pays proper tribute always to Vasari's indispensability as an initial source.

From Milanesi, Horne proceeds to inventories, reconstructing the physical history of the National Gallery painting along with those other paintings, in the Louvre and Uffizi respectively, which constitute a narrative sequence. The London picture, according to Horne, was the best preserved.[14] Such inventories inform us of the earliest location of the sequence, the dimensions of the room where they initially hung, and of the paintings themselves. Horne also details how the paintings were stored, possibly in an attic, exposed to extremes of heat, rain and cold—the Uffizi panel being the most exposed and thus accounting for the varied condition of the three. Horne demonstrates how the confusion of subject in the National Gallery catalogue rose from the compiler assuming that Vasari was describing the San Romano picture when he was actually describing another picture altogether painted on canvas not on panel.

Finally, Horne establishes the precise narrative sequence. The archival evidence is printed at the close of an article written in forcible expository mode and one which has all the vivid logic of a detective story. This is a finely cogent piece and would be sufficient in itself to substantiate a claim for Horne as a scientific art historian of distinction.

"Quelques Souvenirs de Sandro Botticelli," which also appeared during 1901 in the *Revue Archeologique,* is of a miscellaneous character, dealing with disparate Botticellian problems. Horne restores the early *The Adoration of the Magi* to Botticelli's canon. Against Morelli's exclusion of this work, Horne appeals to contemporary tradition, to general internal evidence—the style approximates to that of Botticelli's other juvenilia—and to details, such as the design of hands and the plaits of drapery. Horne also establishes a corrected birth date of 1447 for the master. Moreover, he is placed first in the school of Fillip Lippi and not, as was then believed, in that of Pesellino. Subsequently Botticelli comes under the influence of Pollaiulo.

Horne also adds several other works to the Botticelli canon, including the *Settignano Madonna,* which he appears to have identified in company with Berenson. The thrust of this segment of Horne's piece is to clarify the chronology of Botticelli's early works, recording the transition of the *phillipisant* Botticelli to the Pollaioulesque.[15]

In the article, Horne alludes to himself as having been long engaged with a monograph on Botticelli. On 24 August of that same year, 1901, Mary Berenson wrote to her husband:

"Horne's Botticelli won't be ready for *at least* another year. Horne is in the right to go slowly." Originally the commission from Bell Scott's was dated 1894 and was intended for a modest volume in their Great Masters series.

In his piece on "Botticelli and Nineteenth Century England," Michael Levey informs us that writing on Botticelli in the 1890s was confined to aesthetes and dilettantes. This is not altogether true, as a brief correspondence in the *Academy* indicates.[16] Grant Allen on 3 February 1894 resumes the state of interpretation of the *Primavera*, which follows the traditional Florentine interpretation of the figures: Mercury, the Graces, Venus, Flora "with personifications of Fertility, and a god of wind." It is the reading that Rossetti follows in his sonnet on the painting. Allen replaces this cast with Favonius instead of Mercury and Venus instead of Spring. The Graces are permitted to stay while the three figures on the right of the picture assert themselves as March, April and May. This leads to the conclusion that "it almost looks as if this picture were one of the four panels representing the Four Seasons and I would venture to suggest that each most probably contained in the centre the season it represented. . . . The *Primavera* occupied the first place on the wall so that the figure of March greeted the spectator entering." And analogously to Allen's reading of *Primavera*: "Winter might have had on the right allegorical figures (say Boreas and the Satyrs); and on the left, as if retiring toward the door, the successive figures of December, January and February." Finally Allen asks, "Did Botticelli ever paint any more of the series, for Cosimo de Medici's villa at Castello, or elsewhere?"[17]

Allen was a brilliant dilettante and at least asked some of the right questions. But he was ignorant of archives, of Renaissance neo-Platonism, of the mythographies and of any but the most prominent Renaissance poetry. He was therefore ignorant of the elements that might have furnished and restored the programme. His question about the Castello could have been answered by Vasari, though Vasari, as Horne was to point out in his *Botticelli*, was not above error. Archival material makes it clear that aside from *The Birth of Venus* and the *Primavera*, there were no allegorical pictures at Castello.

The following week Oscar Browning related the *Primavera* to Lucretius's *De Rerum Naturae*, and also to Horace.[18] Horne was to take Lucretius as a prime literary source, but Edgar Wind has defined a compound running back from *La Giostra* to Horace and Ovid's *Fasti* and more faintly to the Lucretian passage. Neither Allen nor Browning allude to the obvious literary source: Poliziano's *La Giostra*, stanzas lxviii-lxx. This was already established, along with Ovid's *Fasti*, by Aby Warburg in his *Sandro Botticelli's Gerbert der Venus und Frubling* (1893).

W. C. F. Anderson, at the time Professor of Classics at Sheffield University College and later Education Officer of Berkshire, had read Warburg, and his refutation of Allen's thesis is complete.[19] Besides *La Giostra*, he cites the *Veris descriptio* and the *Rusticus* of the same author. Anderson continues: "the suggestion that the first three are months is impossible if the central figure is Venus; for April is the Goddess's own month. Spring, as described in the *Hypnerotomachia Poliphili*, closely resembles Botticelli's myth. . . ." Allen had asserted that the figure on the left of the picture was not Mercury, but Favonius (basing this on Horace). But the presence of Favonius is "easily disproved by the passage from Seneca *de beneficiis* 1, 3, quoted by Janitschek, as an explanation of Mercury's presence. . . ." Anderson then brings to bear Cartari's *Le Imagini de i dei degli antiche*, which puts him, as one might say, in a league above Allen and one Oscar Browning. Anderson follows this with the quenching observation "of which unfortunately I only possess a late Paduan celli in the National Gallery is sufficient to suggest "that the central figure is intended for Venus." As for Allen's final suggestion that the picture belonged to a series of all the Four Seasons, Anderson cites Vasari's explicit statements about the painting and Warburg's comments about size.

Whether Horne read Anderson's note we do not know. By the turn of the century he had certainly both corresponded with and met Warburg, putting the great German scholar in touch with Roger Fry and Robert Ross, and exchanging books and information. A letter of 24 July 1903 from 12 Haymarket throws some light on the state of his Botticelli studies at that time. Horne returns Warburg's copy of Alesso Baldovinetti's *Ricordi* and announces that he has found since Warburg left Florence that original *Memoriale* of Franciso Baldovinetti in the Biblioteca Nazionale at Florence. "I am," writes Horne, "printing from it the notices relating to Alesso. The other notices I am printing from the MS copy at the end of your copy of the 'Ricordi'." Among other questions he enquires: "who was de Baudreail for whom the Botticellian tapestry of 'Pallas' reproduced by Muntz was executed for?"[20]

Ross wrote to Berenson on 11 February 1908: "Herbert Horne is looking wonderfully well after his long confinement, and the baby Botticelli is doing very well, though not yet vaccinated by the press. After these perpetual annunciations it is really a great relief to realize that the Messiah is born at last. Horne is quite social and going out into society."[21]

Alessandro Filepepi commonly called Sandro Botticelli Painter of Florence is in folio, designed by the author himself with the usual pale blue Ingres paper cover, end papers of similar hue, and canvas spine with author and title on paper label. Part of the title-page is rubricated, as also are the side notes. In the private press tradition, margins, particularly the base margins, are generous. The paper is handmade and virtually all the pictures were photographed by Emery Walker, who also made and printed the numerous plates. In this great book, Horne's critical method can be viewed at its most elaborate.

His introduction glances at the modern reputation of the master, over accenting the English role in the "rediscovery" of Botticelli during the nineteenth century. His intention, Horne continues, is

> to bring together whatever throws any real light on the life, or work, of Sandro Botticelli, in a historical, antiquarian or aesthetic view; but without losing sight of the fact that the only valuable function of the connoisseur is to distinguish the genuine productions of a master (especially in the case of Sandro) from those of his imitators, and to disengage and note the significant qualities of such genuine works. In a future volume, I propose to discuss the productions both of his immediate disciples and of those painters who fell indirectly under his influence, or who were associated with him in some way or another; in short, the productions of his school in the widest sense of the word. This second volume will, also, contain a catalogue of all the known works of the master and his imitators, and a full index to both volumes.[22]

The second volume was never to be completed; indeed, it was barely assembled, so any judgment on the first must engage with the fact that it is likely to strike the reader as faintly disjunctive in a total impression.

Though Lionello Venturi in his *History of Art Criticism* nowhere directly mentions Horne, it is useful to turn to Venturi's definition of the philological art critic, for it is clearly to such a category that Horne's work broadly belongs.[23] Venturi's attitude to philological critics is negative, though he concedes that the best of such are characterised by a love of art, sensitive drawings, even by lyrical descriptiveness; but this avails them little for philological critics are almost always devoid of hard thinking about the nature of art itself, sharing as they do in that aversion from philosophy fashionable in the second half of the nineteenth century, the period of positivism. This abstention leads, we are told, to a "renunciation of all authentic thought whether historical or philosophical." Still, Venturi admits that the philological critics at least never lose sight of the facts, verifying exact limitations and conditions before judgment. As Reginald Turner said, "Dear Herbert Horne! poring over Botticelli's washing bills—and always a shirt missing."[24]

Historians who are true critics and critics who are true historians, continues Venturi, are "justly irritated" by the philological school because neither iconography nor the history of technique nor the history of abstract figurative elements is the history of art. Art history is quite distinct from all these things and art itself is something nearer to what Hegel saw than to what is seen by the philologist. But, painfully limited though they are, the philological critics are surprisingly found superior to the abstract idealist philosophers who "explain genius rationally" and end by "rationalizing genius." What the philological critic instead explains are the elements of a work of art. Genius, the philological critic ignores; he can indeed only ignore it as one who is convinced that art, that genius, is not reducible to rationality. The function of philological criticism was "*skepticism* with regard to a definition of art like Hegel's which did not take enough account of the nonlogical character of art." And Venturi proceeds by stressing that the true modes of philological criticism—decomposition of sources, virtuosity in attribution (which always requires at least one work by the master on which to base one's deductions) and iconographical research—culminate in research into the individual artist only so that the proper form of philological criticism must be the monograph, the *catalogue raisonée*.

All this has plain implications for books by philological critics, even should they, as does Horne, attempt to deal with a single artist. While no virtuoso in attribution, Horne's book reads in a somewhat atomised fashion, devoid of either generalisations about art or the character of the particular artist, proceeding from painting to painting with much reference here and there to contemporary documents and literature, and with lyrically descriptive panels for the more important works.

Precisely how Horne's *Botticelli* stands in relation to the above definitions may be gathered from Roger Fry's review in the *Burlington Magazine* (1908).[25] Fry was a friend and business associate, besides being eventually the most influential British art critic of his time. It is significant that Fry finds Horne's book to be in some ways old-fashioned. This accords with Venturi's view that philological criticism is largely a nineteenth-century phenomenon. It also edges with a faint irony Fry's praise of the book's physical appearance and of its prose as possessing the qualities of the classic.

First, its leisurely unfolding of material involves the discarding "as modern toys all those methods of abbreviation and co-ordination . . . which writers have gradually elaborated for the greater ease of exposition and as aids to apprehension." The book demands from its reader, Fry tells us, "the same quiet persistence . . . as some folio by Causabon or Diodati." In plainer language it is hard to read both by reason of its ordonnance and its physical size. The knowledge of years is poured out in "one continuous and equable stream" rather like the old man in Wordsworth's "Resolution and Independence." Nevertheless, Fry finds the monumental dignity of the book symptomatic of Horne's general attitude:

> pure science as regards the matter and pure art as regards the presentment. The art critic as a rule adopts neither of these attitudes altogether. Indeed, one scarcely recognises the art critic in Mr. Horne. He gives but little hint of any personal views on aesthetics in general: his technical terms are such as Vasari might have used, or at least would have perfectly understood.

Unlike Venturi's ideal historian of art, or unlike Berenson, of
whom Venturi approved as largely unconcerned with the bare
accumulation of fact, Horne remains

> either incapable or contemptuous of all that delicate analysis of the
> spiritual and temperamental components of a work of art, all that
> subtle exposition of the artist's intention, that illustration of the work
> of art by means of analogy and simile, which make up so large a part
> of the best modern critical literature . . . " It is, indeed, as well done as
> it is possible to imagine"—to phrases almost as simple as this Mr.
> Horne reduces all our elaborate modern apparatus. There is some-
> thing bracing in this austerity, and much truth in the implied condem-
> nation of a great deal of this criticism as too fine drawn, too theore-
> tical, and too liable to personal bias.

At the same time, if Horne stints his audience in this direction,
he is generous, even lavish, in another: "'What is it,' he says,
'that we really know about Simonetta Vespucci?' 'What is it
that we really know?' is a question always in Mr. Horne's mind,
and no efforts are spared either in the task of sweeping away
superincumbent guesswork or in finding out in rough documents what, in fact, we really know." And what was known,
Horne generally tells us, was very little, and often very wrong:

> And in that search no fact seems to Mr. Horne too minute to merit our
> attention, too insignificant to help towards the complete reconstruc-
> tion of the past of Florence of which he perpetually dreams. . . . [He]
> never abbreviates; he seems always to have in view the future his-
> torian, whose gratitude he will earn by the fullness and accuracy of
> his descriptions.

Nonetheless the deliberation with which Horne works, the
length of time his study took to reach the press, brought about
some odd anomalies. The future historian, Fry observes, may
well be puzzled to find Horne anticipating the publication of
Berenson's book on Florentine drawings when that had

appeared four years before the *Botticelli*. And Horne's statement that the programme of Signorelli's *Pan* remains to be discovered reads strangely in view of an article published in the *Monthly Review*, fifth volume of 1901. Horne himself contributed to the same volume, commenting on the puzzling detail of that painting. Fry does not mention the author; it was himself. The details—moon as horn, starry robes, seven pipes—were explained by reference to texts in Macrobius and Servius; but despite an allusion to the fervid neo-Platonism of Lorenzo de Medici and his circle, Fry made no attempt to focus on contemporary Florentine source material. He did not point out that the painting is virtually unique in Signorelli's *oeuvre* but the vague suggestion that there are probably "later Latin" sources seems to suggest that he is not excluding Florentine pantheistic neo-Platonism nor literary texts on the ground of Signorelli's temperament or the type of patron he more usually found. Horne may not have been convinced by the article, or his mode of working may indeed have been such that he did not care for a return to material already composed.

A further feature of Horne's volume lies in his refusal to be satisfied till he has been enabled to visualise each painting precisely as it originally appeared among the surroundings for which it was designed. More than once this exercise leads to valuable suggestions about the painting itself. Fry also points to the presence in the Botticelli volume of what Venturi terms lyrical descriptiveness: "the wonderful use Mr. Horne has made of the now somewhat neglected practice of the verbal descriptions of pictures." With well-known pictures, such verbal description might seem superfluous, but, Fry assures us, frequently some small point is revealed "which one had always overlooked, some readjustment of the relative importance of the parts has been suggested. . . . One can hardly praise enough the admirable literary quality, the directness and beauty of these descriptions." The sensitive eye for detail derives from Ruskin, and from Pater, though Horne's insistence on a contemporary description of Botticelli's figures, their "aria virile," removes from the master that languid and Laodicean image in which Pater had so eloquently imprisoned him.

Horne's caution in attribution leads him in the direction of "demythologising" and he furnished only one new attribution: the damaged fresco of the Annunciation at the suppressed monastery of San Martino in the Via della Scala at Florence. "This book," Fry concludes, "alike in the thoroughness of its scholarship and the gravity of its style has the air of a classic." Ironies and qualifications melt into submissiveness.

Horne himself seems to have been aware of the discontinuous effect of the book—its forward movement checked by repeated enrichment of centrifugal detail. Once he actually observes rather in the manner of a mid-nineteenth-century novelist that "we had broken off our story at the moment when Botticelli had been called to Rome to paint in the Pope's chapel," unless we rather implausibly take this as a device to impose suspense, while the phrase "but to come to the painting" becomes almost formulaic.

A work of such density remains difficult to characterise, difficult even to grasp. It is devoid of sections, chapters, headings and index. Only the side notes afford the reader assistance, and those are contextual references. In practice, the *Botticelli* is generally employed as an encyclopedia, where remarks on individual paintings may be consulted. Perhaps, indeed, it was never intended to be read through at once. But if it were an encyclopedia, then one might reasonably expect more elaborated assistance to the enquirer. As it is, a high proportion of the book is devoted to the drawings related to the *Divine Comedy*, recalling that Horne's taste in collection lay in the direction of the drawing, and not merely in reaction to the Victorian cult of the oil, or the comparative cheapness of

good drawings in the late nineteenth century for the knowl-
edgeable and persistent collector.

Pages again are devoted to the history of Florence after
the death of Il Magnifico in 1492. The power struggles in the
city are, of course, important for Botticelli's career, his loss of
Medicean patronage, his reaction to Savonarola's death and its
putative effect on the final works; but the minuteness with
which Horne enters into the politics of the six years up to
Savonarola's death in 1498 is faintly disproportionate. Still, as
Horne himself might have said, it is time to come to the considerable merits of the book.

It is more accurate to say the *Botticelli* is both an encyclopedia and a rich if oblique personal and aesthetic response to
Sandro's work. The image of Botticelli Horne presents is of a
painter who combines in himself what is best in Florentine
painting of his time, without becoming merely eclectic. For
Horne, Sandro is the unique master of contour, rather than
simply of expressive line: "he invariably uses his line, to
express a definite contour, not only in the outline of the figure,
but of feature, hand, or fold within its mass, and always with a
rhythm and beauty of intention which is unparalleled in Florentine art." This distinguishes Sandro from the "sinewy line" of
Blake and a further distinction is made in discussion of the
painter's "imaginative sensuousness." He is "visionary" but not
"mystic." There is "no trace" of mysticism "in that alert, discriminatory outlook upon the visible world which enables him
to interpret the unseen by the seen, the motive by the action,
the searchings of the heart by a glance of the eye, the gesture
of the hand." Unlike Blake, he is not one who "shuts the eye"
that he may see "things invisible to mortal sight."

Horne in making this judgment rather glides over the two
late works, the *Mystic Nativity* and the *Magdalen at the Foot of
the Cross*, the latter of which he attributed largely to the
Scuoloa. Botticelli, we are told, "elaborates from his subject

with an unfailing dramatic purpose, that variety of motives and attitudes which called forth the admiration of Vasari," a Vasari who was representative of the period that found Botticelli's work in general backward-looking, merely ingenuous. In his attitude to the nude, Sandro exhibits no anatomical curiosity, while in the presentation of suffering he evades the naturalism of his early contemporaries. His *Saint Sebastian* is without any "degradation of pain." The "visionary" quality of the painter's imagination works through not ideal women but recognisable Tuscan types of womanhood, and in discussing the detail of paintings Horne tends to lavish most attention on the female figures. The St. Catherine of the *San Barnaba Altar Piece* has all "the solemn magisterial beauty of gravid women." Elsewhere Horne speaks of "the fruit like grace" of feminine maturity. We are reminded of the lover of Marcellina in his lingering over the Tuscan physical type:

> the long oval of the head, set on the lithe neck and drooping shoulders, the body big in structure and proportions, though angular in form, and heavy at the articulation of the joints and broad, square nails. Even the abundant golden hair, which at first sight might appear a piece of pedantry borrowed from the antique is found to be a Florentine trait.

There are, though, in Sandro's canon occasional reminiscences of antique sculpture.

The book proceeds chronologically, Horne concluding that the Vatican frescoes, overlooked or depreciated because of their proximity to Michelangelo's famous offerings, represent a high point in Sandro's art. The decade between 1482 and 1492 is defined as the time when the painter truly "came into his force." By then that art had become increasingly mannered, the draughtmanship revealing "a more nervous and emphatic delineation of the forms. . . . He had attained the full ripeness of manner, beyond which any further development must, in the nature of things, tend to a deterioration."

Yet Horne admires Botticelli at all periods in his art so that the *Adoration of the Shepherds,* now in the National Gallery, which we might expect to be somewhat unsympathetic to him, relating as it does to that renewal of the Church promised by Savonarola, is described as "the most spiritual, perhaps, and certainly one of the most lovely and imaginative of all Botticelli's works." The praise is deliberately vague as noted by Fry and, less indulgently, by Berenson. Horne makes no attempt to arrange individual paintings in any order of value, and for him the works of the master have an almost equal authority. Discriminatory remarks are mostly confined to suggestions—that a painting has been spoiled by insensitive restoration or by damage; that it does not proceed directly from Botticelli's hand, or only in part; or, inevitably, that it is sometimes the work of imitators merely.

Besides the "aria virile" so often coarsened and sweetened by imitators, a further feature of Sandro's maturity are those characteristic colours, used also to establish the canon, where overpainting or abrasion has not intervened. Fusing clarity with luminosity, they are gemlike in golden hatching, as if with actual sunlight: leaf-greens, olives, golden-browns, grape purples and azures. Horne marks the intensifying severity of Sandro's landscape backgrounds yet remains curiously less alert to an increasing use of architectural contexts to the figures. His rigour in attribution is evident in his refection of superficially attractive works which capture manner, but—like Pater on occasions in his interpretation of the Master—distill delicate feeling into pure sentiment.

Even the rhythmic drama of the two late images of the *Rimpianto di Christo* derive, we are warned, from a sketch of Sandro's, while in the roughly powerful *Magdalen at the Foot of the Cross (Allegria Sacra)* only the saint herself in the feverishly expressive energy of her abandonment is considered to be authentic. The naturalism of the Christ excludes the figure even from the work of the *Scuola* or the imitators. Later criticism tends to react against such radical disintegrationism.

In the conclusion, Horne defines his relationship to the two great English critics who rediscovered Botticelli for a wider public: Ruskin and Pater. Both mediate a highly personalised image of the master, over-accenting elements that are indeed present but in pure solution. Ruskin reacted to a certain "strange hardness and gloom," that "aria virile," so admired by Botticelli's contemporaries and by Vasari, which appeared to one who took the gentler virtues of English landscape painters and the English Pre-Raphaelites as his norm of judgment. Pater, on the other hand, detected "a sentiment of ineffable melancholy," thus establishing an antithesis to Ruskin's Botticelli. And it was Pater's image which predominated in the *fin de siècle*. But a major element in the work, the consequence of Botticelli's temperament, evaded both. That temperament was typically Florentine and his art constantly "reveals the ever-shifting colours of the Florentine temperament . . . the keen sense of expressive beauty, the bizarre imagination, the amatorious sweetness and tenderness of the age in which he lived," a strangeness in beauty which Horne distinguishes from the willed oddity of later Florentine painters such as Pontormo and Il Rosso. Yet Sandro's work displays also, as the later pictures witness, much of the feeling which is more distinctively characteristic of an earlier age of Florentine art:

> If, like Dante, he can faint with love, he inherits, in common with the naturalistic painters, no small portion of the virility, the energy, the directness, and at times the gloom, or even some tincture of the cruelty of the Florentine temperament; qualities which live for all time in the *Divina Comedia* . . . the current obverse and reverse of the Florentine character.

Horne deduces the bizarre, unexpected element in Sandro's personal character from the capriciousness, whimsicality, almost practical joking that the scattered anecdotes of the master suggest.

The major set-pieces of writing in the volume are the prose descriptions of the allegory of *Primavera* and *Nascita di Venere*. The second of these may be quoted extensively to suggest affinities with Horne's master, Pater:

> The Goddess, amid a shower of roses, stands naked in the little bark of the shell, in the attitude of the Medicean Venus. On the left of the picture, two winged zephyrs blow hard across the gray water, moving forward the dainty-lipped shell on which she sails; the sea "showing his teeth" on thin lines of foam, and sucking in one by one the falling roses, each severe in outline, plucked off short at the stalk, but embrowned a little, as Botticelli's roses always are. On the other side, a nymph, in an ample dress of white, powdered with sprigs of corn-cockle, having a wreath of myrtle about the neck, and girdled about the waist with rose-branches, steps forward on the shore, ready to cast a purple cloak, sprinkled with knots of daisies, about the naked goddess, as soon as she shall step to land. The orange trees are in flower; and along the water's edge, the distant shore juts out into little promontories in the clear morning air.

Horne then proceeds to quote appositely some five and a half stanzas from Poliziano's *La Giostra* and from a Greek epigram of the same poet, which itself looks back to the Greek Anthology. In its Latin translation, Poliziano's epigram has the phrase "tegebat pubem"—a departure from the iconography of Apelles's painting, central to the tradition of representing the Love Goddess wringing out her hair with both hands. In another type of antique sculpture, though, Venus appears with legs draped, one hand screening her bosom, the other covering the pubes. In this controlled use of visual sources Horne notes the differences between Poliziano's and Botticelli's response to the incident. Where Poliziano "recovers the story as a scholar from out the vestige of the vanished Greek world, relying on the felicity of phrase or the beauty with which he turns a familiar image," the painter

> ever careful of that tradition of naturalism, which, for him, is an inseparable part of his art, seeks to refashion the legend out of his vision of the sensuous world around him, of what is "here and now." In place of the "stormy Aegean" Botticelli paints the water which has given birth to this damsel of more than human mould, as he may have seen it on his way to Rome, at Trasimeno, or Bolsena. The low, grassy dunes run down to the edge of the water which breaks under the light winds, into little waves among the bullrushes at the shore, only to stretch away at the horizon, serene and motionless as the sky above it. In the nude figure of the Venus Botticelli is careful to preserve the expressive, rather than beautiful, Tuscan type as he found it at Florence.

There follows the description already cited of that type, concluding with the judgment that

> all these lineaments and characters . . . become in this figure of Venus transfigured by the sentiment of which they are themselves the expression. Clad in the proper robes of the gods, this "Donzella" wears her garments of nakedness like some cloistral habit; and comes on with a high, ineffable blytheness, which savours rather of the circles of Paradise, than of the heights of Olympus.

The use of the present tense, the interior rhymes, expressive epithets and the modulation of sentences—particularly that sentence describing the dunes running toward the horizon, so arranged as to suggest that both sand and water stretch to the western limits of the eye—all belong to the nineteenth-century tradition of discovering the significance of a work in the impression that its formal aspects make.

This species of prose has been acutely analysed for use in G. Robert Stange's "Art Criticism as a Prose Genre," stressing how in such writing the effects of rhythm and tone translate into kinetic activity, into synaesthetic effects, as though the sentence was a plastic form no less than muscular response.[26] However, the cold excitement behind Horne's evocation of the "Donzella" is checked at once by a deliberately objective tone:

> The colour, "cadaverous, or at least cold," which Pater noticed in the picture, is partly due to the fact that the medium, the glair and yolk of egg, with which the pigments were tempered, has much deteriorated in consequence of the canvas on which the picture is painted, and partly because the picture has not been varnished.

Thus preserved against damp, the surface suffers from over-cleaning rather than repainting. The critic then proceeds to inform us that the execution is not everywhere equal to the conception, particularly in the treatment of draperies.

In the first part of the opening description, the quotation from *The Renaissance* melts rhythmically and tonally into its new context. The cunning epithet "cadaverous" by which obliquely, perhaps subliminally, Pater suggests his general interpretation of Botticelli's temperament is by tonic anti-climax reduced, though not abolished by the detached look at the colour effects and the state of the canvas that follow.

In the last analysis, Pater and Horne are not so far apart in their impression of the painting's effect: what Pater terms "mediaeval," Horne more precisely describes as "Giottesque" while Pater's point about Botticelli's work representing the Greek spirit to a greater degree for us than the best work of the Greeks themselves is elaborated by Horne. Elsewhere, though, Pater is criticized for a too liberal interpretation of the possible heretical effects implicit in the Tondo of the Magnificat. Like Pater, Horne delights in extended, elegant translation from literary sources. As I have suggested above, like Pater, too, he isolates the "Greek" and "Modern" elements in Sandro, rejoic-ing in fusions between Greek and Christian: so, the allusions to the "cloistral" Venus, aware as her "tagebat pubem" wit-nesses, of shame, the Fall, even before the Incarnation, as she coasts landward from the glittering sperm of her origin. Here, as nearly always, though the personal response is subduedly present, the painting is barely related to Botticelli's psychology. The object is finally isolated as far as possible from its creator, but also, unlike Pater, left free-standing, from its critic.

It remains to be asked, why should Horne have so rapidly abandoned that second volume of the Botticelli which was to have comprised an index, *catalogue raisonnée* and discussion of the "School" and the imitators? After a dozen arduous years at least with Sandro, he may have sensed that he was doing no more than elaborating norms and judgments explicit and implicit already established in the completed work. A deeper reason perhaps lay in the fact that the focus of this critical and archival interest had shifted to the period in which Botticelli came to maturity, to the early and middle fifteenth century in Florence, precisely as Horne had moved from Wren to Inigo Jones to Vitruvius. His last published article on Botticelli's *Last Communion of Saint Jerome* also reveals that his attention had veered from the painting to questions of ownership, genealogy, and the Florentine archives. Any one of the books he is recorded as planning after 1910 would have taken a decade of painful work, and that work was perhaps more formally appropriate in the bare presentation of documents.

CHAPTER **8**

The Final Phase

Although not precisely in the world of connoisseurs, art historians and dealers, Reginald Turner, like Rothenstein, saw as much of Horne as anyone during Horne's last years. Turner indeed presents an image of Horne in his novel *Samson Unshorn* (1909). Horne appears as Jasper Fawn who shocks a British aristocrat by laughing at a large canvas of the Holy Family. The good Lord protests that the picture is not funny when Fawn defends himself by employing his favourite word, "amusing." Fawn's only other comments on paintings are "rotten" or "good." The generalised epithets of the *Botticelli* can be seen as extensions of Horne's informal judgments. His laugh, we are told, "was the terror of the auctioneer. His laugh had been known to stop the bidding for a picture when the price was leaping up, and he caused hitherto supposed masterpieces to be bought in, costing the owners several thousand pounds." Fawn's character certainly closely resembles that of Horne: "He had no raging desire for notoriety. His position was too unassailable and his ideas too fixed. Moreover, not to be well known was useful when he came to pick up a bargain or to sift a jewel from the rubbish."[1]

In his article in the *Anglo-Italian Review*, Turner speaks of Horne as "grim . . . almost sullen in manner until he thawed,

145

and then he had a very distinct and powerful charm." We are also told that Horne used to make "occasional predatory visits to London," particularly to the area of the Fulham Road: "there it was that he picked up two of Michelangelo's original sketches for the Sistine Chapel for a penny each." We may assume this to be typical, if not actual truth.

Max Beerbohm in his letters to Turner summons up Horne and "The Laugh":

> when did you begin to be this austere Florentine *dilettante?* Did the shade of Herbert Horne accompany you on your visits to the curio-shops, frowning and nudging, and uttering some faint echo of that hoarse raven laugh which meant "spurious"?[2]

Horne is also present briefly in another of Turner's novels, *Count Florio and Phyllis K.* (1910), and Max duly explains to his wife "the nature of Herbert Horne" so as to accentuate for her the fun of the characterisation: "I wonder if . . . H. H. 'had his attention drawn' to the book. . . . he would be wounded to the core."[3]

In a letter dated 10 February (presumably 1913)[4] Turner informed Beerbohm that

> Horne moves into his palace soon, which may mean in about three months. At any rate his books are being transplanted. I have got one or two bits of furniture from him which do not suit his palace and which he wanted to get rid of, and he is having some Empire chairs— which are not very pretty but which he says are good—covered for me.[5]

It was at this time also that Horne sent Randall Davies the fruit of his twenty-year research into the poems and letters of the Earl of Rochester in the hope that Davies would complete the edition. Yet although he was distinctly out of touch with the latest shudders in English works of literature and art, he showed some mild interest in Davies's account of the Camden

Town school and in the rise of Wyndham Lewis. Indeed, his reference to Lewis is, in terms of documentation, an early one. On 14 April 1914, he sent Davies a copy of

> our Florentine "Futurist" Magazine. Please read carefully the first article "contro le Donne" and give special attention to the first design by Rosai. Tho' I fear you are not sufficiently Florentine to grasp the full import of the fragments of words and other things which figure in that remarkable drawing. . . . I wish you would pass it on to Wyndham Lewis, and tell him that I should be so very grateful to know how he and his school would treat such a subject. I imagine his friezes for the dining rooms of the great, culminate with a specially attractive treatment of the same theme.[6]

The magazine is *Lacerba*. The article by Giovanni Papini is entitled "Il Massacro delle Donne" and the subject of Rosai's drawing is "Latrina."[7]

In 1912, Horne purchased a decayed Florentine palazzo at 6 Via dei Benci with the purpose of creating a context for his collections. The Conte Gamba observes:

> In course of time he began restricting his purchases . . . making it his particular purpose to collect ancient objects of household use, which if not always worthy of a place in a larger museum were such as to display the practical sense and decorative taste of the rare objects . . . which have formed part of the traditional furnishing of a house belonging to the ancient Florentine bourgeoisie.[8]

These objects included furnishing of massive walnut in pure style and plain good taste, ceramic ware of the best factories for the table, and humbler but typical and attractive objects of household use, as well astrolabes, surgical instruments and chests with arabesqued Florentine work. According to Gamba:

> The ancient palace of the Alberti, at the corner of the Corso dei Tintori and the Via dei Benci, was purchased by the Corsi family in 1489 and most probably was re-built by them in its present form after drawings by Giuliano da San Gallo. Although this is not proved by

any existing document, seeing the fruitless researches made by Horne
himself in the archives of that family, stylistic reason and comparison
with other constructions and ornamentations by that celebrated
architect, specially with the Gondi Palace, point to such a conclusion.

The artist had evidently proposed showing how a house of small
size could be made splendid and elegant by means of the art of
proportion, distribution of light and sober and studied ornamentation. Above a large and light underground he succeeded in raising
three floors of spacious rooms, with access by a wide and rich stair, at
the same time providing several conveniences not common in ancient
constructions.

The exterior, surrounded at the base by that inviting stone bench,
which almost exclusively at Florence, seems to uphold, and ennoble,
the principal palaces of the Renaissance, attracts the gaze on account
of the harmonious distribution of stone and space. The courtyard has
but a single portico, which however is spacious and has slender
columns with capitals and consoles, all of different design, and friezes
of foliage over the doors carved with the utmost delicacy by
Giuliano's best stone-workers, perhaps with assistance of Andrea
Sansoviano himself, as may be argued from analogous capitals in the
sacristy of the Church of Santo Spirito. Below the two rows of inside
window run fascie of graffito. The stair overlooks the courtyard from
two slender-columned loggie; while on a third floor it overlooks the
whole of this restricted vertical prospect from the third covered but
sunny loggia. In ancient times it was used for drying the wools which
are dyed in the laboratories in the basement, for the trade carried on
by the industrious ancient owners, who probably had their office or
warehouse in the ground-floor rooms, still admirable on account of
the rich consoles of the vaults. Here there was once, it would seem, a
fine chimney-piece of carved stone, while another very rich one
adorned a room on the first floor, over the door of which ran friezes
in the same taste and skilful workmanship as those below. But all this,
alas, was sold in days past, and some pieces are known which now
serve as examples of ornamentation in Institutions across the Ocean.
On the other hand, the wonderful figured console in the courtyard,
that upholds the vault of the loggia, and which had been removed a
great many years before, was munificently given back by Prof.
Stefano Bardinoi to the Horne Museum.

Once in the possession of this precious edifice, the worthy
learned Englishman devoted himself to restoring it to its ancient state
and appearance, removing partitions and overlayings, freeing rail-

ings, bringing to light again the original plastering both within and without, restoring the stone-work and reconstructing doors and window-panes according to the ancient traces discovered.[9]

In the old Corsi palace, Horne lived frugally, in one room virtually at the top of the building, sitting, so one account runs, in a cane chair in what served both as a library and a bedroom. Papers might be kept in the massive chests below, but otherwise the *piano nobile* and the floor above were given over to pictures, statuary, and cabinets for drawings.

The little room upstairs was all that remained to Horne and the twentieth century. Here he lived for the last two years of his life in declining health, without electric light or continuous hot water supply, since these services were not appropriate to the building. From the severest art-historical point of view, the only inappropriate item in the house was Horne himself.

For most of his life Horne appears to have suffered from ill health. His letters are full of references to colds, influenza, and mysterious debilities. His health became alarming in 1912 and by 1914 he had consulted seven Florentine doctors in addition to his own regular physician. Work in the palazzo was still unfinished when his condition became critical. After three days of acute pain he died on 14 April 1916.

During his long periods of ill health, when much of his time had to be spent in bed, people came to his house bringing objects to offer him for purchase. Even in the last few hours of his life the ruling passion was active: he summoned up sufficient strength to acquire the *Saint Catherine* of Luca Signorelli.

We have further glimpses of the final scene from Reginald Turner's letters to his old friend Randall Davies, whom Horne had appointed literary executor:

> Two days before he died Herbert sent for me to give me several
> bundles of papers which he asked me to destroy without looking at. .
> . . They were no doubt private papers which concerned no one but
> himself. . . . . He showed me a book which contained a MS, poems
> written recently by him, and this you will no doubt have in due time.[10]

Of this volume, there is no trace in the archives of the Museo
Horne, nor does it appear in the collection of Mrs. T. C.
Dugdale, who inherited Horne's personal papers from her first
husband, Randall Davies. It may be that the manuscripts of
earlier poems in the Museo Horne were what Turner had in
mind, for those include unpublished poems, though few if any
appear to date from after 1900. Turner continues:

> I saw a good deal of Herbert during his last months, much more than
> any one else, and though as you know he was not expansive by
> nature, he often spoke of you with great affection. He suffered a great
> deal at the end but bore all with wonderful fortitude and remained
> always occupied and interested, and I don't think he in the least
> expected to die, till a week or less before he did die. He seems never
> to have thought of making a will and it all had to be done in a hurry. It
> was after he made the will that he asked me to destroy certain papers
> and he showed perfect lucidity and great strength at that interview
> although he was at the point of death.[11]

Horne's will, it appears from Turner's account, was also
drawn up unsatisfactorily by an Italian lawyer and it may be
that the odd distribution of Horne's remains between the
municipality of Florence and the collection of Mrs. Dugdale
was the consequence. The letters to Horne from Ernest
Dowson clearly came under the head of personal papers and
should therefore have come into the possession of the literary
executor but, like the manuscripts of the earlier poems,
remained in the Casa Horne. Other literary material may well
have disappeared.

His collections Horne bequeathed to the Italian state. His
intention had been that these should be added to, but his

Italian friends, who had the disposition of the sums he left for the upkeep of the Museo Horne, invested much money in Italian State Bonds which disastrously depreciated. Few visitors in the 1920s and 1930s visited the Museo. In the post-war period it was more or less permanently closed. I was fortunate to come into contact with the custodian, Signor Tito Messeri, son of Horne's housekeeper, who cherished the memory of the great collector and art historian and gave me free access to the house and its contents. A few years after my visit, the drawings, including the English water-colours and a superb sketchbook of Tiepolo, were moved to the Uffizi.

According to Maurice Brockwell, "those who are in a high position to know believe that he left much literary material of a high quality including finished manuscripts for books on Pesellino and Bianca Capello." Moreover, Lee Warner of the Riccardi Press remarked in a letter to Davies of 29 April 1916: "I have not seen him since 1913. We then had a long discussion, succeeding others in the previous year, as to a revised version of his Leonardo, the completion of his Botticelli and separate lives from Vasari completely annotated. [There was] also a terrific work on the (I think) Riccardi Palace." No trace of the complete manuscripts of those appears to remain.[12]

The memoir which Randall Davies contributed to the exhibition of Horne's English paintings held in the autumn of 1916 was based on a typewritten lecture which exists in two versions, the first annotated by Horne's sister, Beatrice. Davies, who was one of Horne's intimate friends, offers several valuable observations on Horne:

> Even in his earliest work, when he was only just of age, there was "a strength and warrantise of skill" that promised much more, if people had only seen it, than some of the more brilliant and taking beginnings of many of his contemporaries.[13]

Davies also gives us details of yet another of Horne's unfinished works,

> an exhaustive study of Cozens which was to have been printed in the
> Burlington Magazine. "You will be glad to hear" began one of his
> letters to me just over a year ago, "that the Anglo-Russian alliance is
> shortly to have a leg-up and the world in general is to be informed
> how Peter the Great was the founder, in every sense of the word, of
> the British School of Water Colour Painting. Of course you and I
> know that it all came about through Alexander C."[14]

And contradicting what Image was reported to have said to Symons:

> "I think I am the only one of my generation," he said to me once,
> "who has not been influenced by Oscar Wilde." And that aloofness—
> not social by any means, but in his work—was one of the secrets of
> his more solid if less brilliant success. Not only did he not seek
> popular recognition; he positively avoided it.[15]

And of the collections in the Palazzo:

> Each drawing is mounted by his own hand, and on the back of each is
> written by him the account from which the following catalogue is
> compiled. Here, as in all that he did, one may discern the spirit of that
> marginal note of Inigo Jones's that Horne was so fond of quoting—"In
> the name of God, Amen."[16]

Fritz Saxl's description of Horne remains definitive:

> Herbert Horne's outlook in his earlier years was widely intellectual
> and specifically English; he painted Pre-Raphaelite allegories, he
> wrote poetry, edited seventeenth-century texts, collected English
> water-colours, was a member of a guild . . . and a friend of the
> Rossettis, of Oscar Wilde, and Walter Pater. He said about himself in
> those early years: "in no-one on earth (I am conceited here) is 'the
> torrid and the frigid interwove' more than I." At a certain point he left
> England with all her friendly figures, gave up his work as an artist and
> a man of letters, and became an austere Florentine scholar who rather

shunned the company of men. His main interest in life was from then on to write on Botticelli accurately and disinterestedly in a frigid style which almost obliterates the personality of the author. Any attempt to connect the effects of Botticelli's art with his own emotional experience is so severely avoided—an almost heroic attempt at subduing the "torrid" streak in his character in order to produce an unimpeachable piece of historical scholarship.[17]

To this one might add that Florence rather than Botticelli became his main interest in life. But the style indeed became the man—or the man the style. Other mentors, too, might have been mentioned: Mackmurdo, Image, Stewart Headlam, and Morris, who affected Horne as he affected many in Horne's generation. Yet Horne though angrily aware of the role of capital in the destruction of the past, of amenities, of buildings and of townscapes, was virtually a man without politics, even if in earlier years he was faintly attracted through Image and Headlam to a species of Christian Socialism, one that saw the flesh as sacramentalised rather than corrupt.

Horne's relationship with Oscar Wilde is more puzzling. The two men probably came to know one another in 1886 and a dozen or so letters were exchanged between that date and 1891. Wilde contributed to the *Century Guild Hobby Horse* and the two were associated in an abortive scheme to place a plaque designed by Horne in Chatterton's old school at Bristol. However, Wilde's projected essay on Chatterton for the *Century Guild Hobby Horse*, an elaborate affair, was abandoned half-finished. Wilde wrote warmly to Horne about a presentation copy of *Diversi Colores,* but there the record ends. Their interests, their ambiances diverged, though not altogether so. For Horne remained friendly with Wilde's circle, survivors such as Ross, Turner, Beerbohm. It was certainly no simple ethical choice.

From the beginning, Horne had been charmed by Wilde. The man and his letters have the same warmly naïve, almost boyish note that we find in Lionel Johnson's letters at the time of a first encounter with the great aesthete: "Oscar has asked me to tea tomorrow and wrote a most complimentary letter about my verse." Or "I dine with him tomorrow. Mrs. O. is about 22 and very very very very very very [illegible]—so now you know." It is only Symons who suggests any overt homosexuality in Horne. The exclusive (and vulgar) relationship with Lord Alfred Douglas isolated Horne, as it isolated John Gray and Johnson, from Wilde. We have a last splendid glimpse in a letter of Horne to Rhys from 20 Fitzroy Street on 9 February 1890: "I asked the Rhymers here the other evening: Oscar came in at the end, after the rhymes were all over, and smiled like a Neronian Apollo upon us all. A kind of enthusiasm or inspiration followed."[18]

In the manner somewhat of Yeats, Horne submitted to many mentors, then dismissed them as mentors, though not necessarily as friends, when he had exhausted what they had to offer. By their influence, he released in himself potentialities, brought them to definition, by a series of disgusts, as Pater wrote of Leonardo da Vinci, rather than by the alienation and synthetic process that we find in Yeats. Superficially this may recall Wilde's notions of the instability of the self, the multiplication of selves; but Horne's terminology of "torrid" and "frigid" suggests an act of self-transparency. Pater's practice, if not Pater's doctrine, furnished the model.

Puzzling, unsympathetic, contained, faintly sinister even, are the epithets that others found appropriate to Horne's personality. The final impression remains of a man embarrassed by a multiplicity of competing talents, who gradually liberates himself by quiet and firm acts of will. The *Hobby Horse,* in which one may trace that movement toward the "frigid," the intensifying antiquarian and archival note, his poetry, and his decorative work were virtually abandoned. There follows a process of self-purification that extends to the private life. The final architectonic idea, one might say, was a classicism of personality.

That enthusiastic and speculative youth who had impressed Image, so generous in emitting general ideas, transformed himself by the age of twenty-five into the tired, finicky, silent presence evoked by "Michael Field" and angering John Davidson. It is not sufficient to stress the ever-increasing specialising of interest, the caution of the semi-invalid who must preserve his energies. As his own iconography witnesses: in the portrait by H. Harris Brown of 1908, reproduced in the *Catalogue of the Horne Museum*, the full lips, the clairvoyant fingers as they stroke objects for texture, plainly indicate that though sublimated the "torrid vein" remained.

Notes

CHAPTER 1   The Early Phase

1. Information about Horne must necessarily be culled from diverse sources. Randall Davies's introduction to *The Burlington Fine Art Club Exhibition of Mr. Herbert Horne's Collection of Drawings* . . . (1916). Mary Berenson's *éloge* in *Rassegna D'Arte*, 16 (1916), p. 10, is too brief to be of strong interest, though it is agreeable to be assured that Horne was "ultimo amico" of both Morris and Pater.

Others which are of interest: Reginald Turner, "Herbert Horne," *Anglo-Italian Review*, 2:6 (October 1918), pp. 154-59. E. W. Anthony, "The Horne House, Florence," *House Beautiful*, 52 (November 1922), pp. 413-16. Arthur Symons, "The Hobby Horse," *Vanity Fair*, 17 (1922), p. 54. A. J. Rusconi, "The Horne Collection in Florence," *Connoisseur*, 63 (May 1922), pp. 3-13. Conte Gamba, "Il Palazzo della Raccolta Horne a Firenze," *Dedalo*, 1 (1925). Dudley Habron, "Minor Masters of the Nineteenth Century. Notes on some lesser known architects. VIII. Herbert Horne, the Critic as Artist," *Architectural Review*, 81 (January-June 1937), pp. 32-33. For information on Max's caricature of Horne, see *A Catalogue of the Caricatures of Max Beerbohm*, Rupert Hart-Davis, comp. (Cambridge: Harvard University Press, 1972), p. 79. See also Charles G. Harper, *English Pen Artists of To-Day. Examples of Their Work. Some Criticism and Appreciations* (London: Percival, 1892), pp. 84-85. There are some brilliant pages in Fritz Saxl, *Lectures* (London: Warburg Institute, University of London, 1957), pp. 332-35.

A few autobiographical details occur in the preface by Horne provided for Randall Davies's *Chelsea Old Church* (London: Duckworth 1904), pp. xi-xiv: "At Chelsea the writer and myself first learned to spell together, as boys, the elements of antiquarian lore. How far into the past this first small incursion has led us to wander—into what regions of arts and letters—this is not the place to recount, were it worth the telling. But we have always returned to Chelsea, our 'alma mater', with gratitude and with devotion." Horne is mentioned in numerous memoirs of the late Victorian and Edwardian eras.

2. Horne's sister, Beatrice, was a distinguished performer on the viol with Arnold Dolmetsch.

3. Reginald Turner, *Anglo-Italian Review* (October 1918), p. 153.

4. See, Ian Fletcher, "Bedford Park: Aesthete's Elysium?" in *Romantic Mythologies* (London: Routledge & Kegan Paul, 1967), pp. 169-207.

5. William Morris Museum, Walthamstow, MS Century Guild 192/15.

6. This and the following extracts are from the archives of the Museo Horne, Florence.

CHAPTER 2   Horne and Some Contemporaries

1. See Ernest Rhys's *Everyman Remembers* (London: J. M. Dent, 1931), pp. 94-97, and *Wales England Wed: An Autobiography by Ernest Rhys* (London: J. M. Dent, 1940), pp. 80-82. Herbert's younger brother, Louis, had invited Rhys to hear a long and strange poem on Saint John the Divine and in the middle of the reading accusing Rhys of not listening, burst out of the room. There followed a desperate chase by Herbert round London until Louis was finally discovered in a cheap lodging-house. After several similar crises, Louis was shipped off to Canada to pursue an open-air life. He made partial recovery, though he seems to have been under medical attention to the end of his life. Louis was also attracted to the visual arts and Rhys recalls looking at his strange visionary paintings in the Blake tradition. For discussion of Beatrice Horne, see Mabel Dolmetsch, *Personal Recollections of Arnold Dolmetsch* (London: Routledge, 1958).

2. From a MS, formerly in the possession of Miss Elinor Pugh.

3. *Works and Days, from the Journal of Michael Field*, T. and D. C. Sturge Moore, eds. (London: John Murray, 1933), pp. 118, 121.

4. Edgar Jepson, *Memoirs of a Victorian* (London: Victor Gollancz, 1933), pp. 222-23.

5. The typescript at Princeton, "A Study in Morbidity: Herbert Horne," has been published in *The Memoirs of Arthur Symons: Life and Art in the 1890s*, Karl Beckson, ed. (University Park and London: Pennsylvania State University Press, 1977), pp. 125-28.

6. Horne's passport in the archives of the Museo Horne, Florence, reveals him to have been five feet ten inches in height.

7. This was William Llewelyn Hacon, Charles Ricketts's partner in the Vale Press. Hacon, son of William Mackmurdo Hacon, married Edith Caherne Broadbent, 21, daughter of John Broadbent, on 14 February 1895 at the Register Office, District of Westminster, Selwyn Image and his wife to be, being the witnesses. Hacon died on 23 July 1910 and Phyllis on 25 August 1952. Horne, in fact, seems to have assisted Hacon's courtship of Miss Broadbent.

8. This and subsequent letters from typescript copies of the correspondence in my possession. The location of the originals is not known to me.

9. See, for example, "Pages from the Life of Murel Broadbent, Original Preface," typescript, Princeton University, and "The Life and Adventure of Murel Broadbent," Arizona State University.

10. *Under the Hill* (Paris: Olympia Press, 1959), pp. 40-46. For a more detailed discussion of Beardsley's novel, see my "Inventions for the Left Hand: Beardsley in Verse and Prose," in *Reconsidering Aubrey Beardsley*, Robert Langenfeld, ed. (Ann Arbor and London: UMI Research Press, 1989), 227-66.

CHAPTER 3   The Poet and His Poetry

1. For an account of these halls, see Mark Edwards Perugini, *Victorian Days and Ways* (London: Jarrolds, 1964). Also see Ralph Nevill, *The Gay Victorians* (London: E. Nash & Grayson, 1930); Ivor Forbes Guest, *The Alhambra Ballet* (Brooklyn, NY: Dance Perspectives, Inc., 1959); Ivor Forbes Guest, *The Empire Ballet* (London: Society of Theatre Research, 1962).

2. Sources are manuscripts in the archives of the Museo Horne, Florence; William Morris Gallery, Walthamstow; the Bodleian Library; and magazines such as the *Church Reformer, Soho Parish Magazine*, the *Hobby Horse* and the *Century Guild Hobby Horse*.

3. See Loraine Rose Lively Hunt, "*The Century Guild Hobby Horse*: A Study of a Magazine." Ph.D. Dissertation, University of North Carolina (1965), pp. 95-101, in particular.

4. The form was practiced by Cartwright, Lluelyn and other seventeenth-century poets, and by such contemporaries of Horne as Image, Lionel Johnson, and John Gray. Johnson had reservations about the sincerity of poems of this order by such suavely agnostic Anglicans as Horne and Image.

5. Archives of the Museo Horne, Florence.

CHAPTER 4   The Craftsman and Architect

1. In a letter to Dudley Harbron, now in the William Morris Gallery. See the Appendix for a list of Horne's designs.

2. *Nero and Other Plays*. Herbert P. Horne, Havelock Ellis, Arthur Symons and A. Wilson Verity, eds. (London: T. F. Unwin, 1888).

3. For Pater, an early influence, Horne preserved the highest respect, and Pater's initials, along with those of Brightwell, compose the dedication of Horne's book on Botticelli. Several American scholars, such as Loraine Rose Lively Hunt, state with sedulous rashness that the *Century Guild Hobby Horse* and the *Hobby Horse* reacted against Pater, whom they casually subsume under the rubric "art for art's sake." Pater's work is twice enthusiastically reviewed in the pages of these periodicals. Galton had initial reservations, but these were finally dispelled.

4. Fritz Saxl, *Lectures* (London: Warburg Institute, University of London, 1957), p. 334.

5. E. 1147 and E. 1151-1920. A new house for the caretaker is included.

6. Bodley. MS Eng. letters. e 38. f. 69.

7. See *The Life and Letters of Frederic Shields*, Ernestine Mills, ed. (London: Longmans, Green & Co., 1912), p. 306. Also see *The Letters of Emelia Russell Gurney*, Ellen Mary Gurney, ed. (London: J. Nisbet, 1902), pp. 270-82.

8. *The Life of Percy Dearmer*, Nancy Dearmer, ed. (London: Jonathan Cape, 1940), pp. 78-79, 91.

9. Victoria and Albert Museum, E. 1136-1920. A relatively detailed account of Horne's programme survives among his papers in the possession of Mrs. T. C. Dugdale.

10. These are among Mrs. T. C. Dugdale's collection.

11. From Beatrice Horne's comments on Randall Davies's brief memoir of Horne, both MSS in the collection of Mrs. T. C. Dugdale.

12. In his autobiographical notes, now is the William Morris Gallery, Walthamstow, Mackmurdo lays no claim to the design of Savoy Hotel, though it is difficult to believe that he was not in some way involved.

13. Victor Plarr tells us that Arthur Galton also had rooms, see *Ernest Dowson 1888-1897: Reminiscences, Unpublished Letters and Marginalia* (London: Elkin Mathews, 1914), p. 68.

14. Letter to Miss E. M. Pugh, 6 May 1942, in the William Morris Gallery Walthamstow. For other brief descriptions of the "Fitzroy Settlement," see *Works and Days, from the Journal of Michael Field*, T. and D. C. Sturge Moore, eds. (London: John Murray, 1933), p. 117; and Victor Plarr, *Ernest Dowson*, pp. 63-64, 67-69.

CHAPTER 5   Crucial Years as Editor

1. "Mr. A. H. Mackmurdo and The Century Guild," *Studio*, 16 (1899), p. 187.

2. "*William Blake's Marriage of Heaven and Hell*, now first printed from the engraved original, with an Introductory Note by the Editor," *Century Guild Hobby Horse*, 2 (1887), p. 135.

3. Ibid., p. 136.

4. "The Book of Los: By William Blake, 1795; With an Introduction by F. York Powell," *Century Guild Hobby Horse*, 5 (1890), pp. 82-83.

5. "Some Considerations of the Nature of Fine Art: Being a Paper Read Before the Students of the Whitechapel Craft School, in Little Alie Street, on the 26th of April, MDCCCXCI," *Century Guild Hobby Horse*, 6 (1891), pp. 84-85.

6. Loraine Rose Lively Hunt, "*The Century Guild Hobby Horse*: A Study of a Magazine." Ph.D. Dissertation, University of North Carolina (1965).

7. "A Study of Inigo Jones," *Century Guild Hobby Horse*, 1 (1886), p. 123.

8. Archives of the Museo Horne, Florence.

9. Lilian Block, "*The Pursuit of Beauty*: The Background and Creators of the Hobby Horse Magazine," M.A. Dissertation, Columbia University (1965), p. 145.

10. British Library, Add. MS 46363.

11. From a letter in the possession of Professor A. W. Patrick.

12. Ibid.

13. *Spirit Lamp*, June 1893, p. 70.

14. "In Praise of Youth. Lionel Johnson," *Century Guild Hobby Horse*, 5 (1890), p. 141.

15. From letter in the possession of Professor A. W. Patrick.

16. "William Bell Scott, Poet, Painter, and Critic: Born 12 September, 1811; Died 22 November, 1890," *Century Guild Hobby Horse*, 6 (1891), p. 27.

17. *Century Guild Hobby Horse*, 6 (1891), p. 14.

18. Ibid., p. 61-67.

19. From letter in the possession of Professor A. W. Patrick.

20. *The Letters of Ernest Dowson*, Desmond Flower and Henry Maas, eds. (London: Cassell, 1967), p. 190. The letter is undated and March 1891 has been provisionally assigned.

21. Letter in the collection of Mrs. T. C. Dugdale.

22. "A Brief Notice of Edward Calvert, Painter and Engraver," *Century Guild Hobby Horse*, 6 (1891), p. 116.

23. Ibid. p. 135.

24. From letter in the possession of Professor A. W. Patrick.

25. From letter in the collection of Mrs. T. C. Dugdale.

26. "A Preface," *Century Guild Hobby Horse*, 4 (1889), p. 7.

27. The full title is actually "Notes on the 'Quadriregio' of Federico Frezzi, by Richard Garnett, to Which are Prefixed Some Remarks upon the Principles of Wood-Cutting," *Century Guild Hobby Horse*, 3 (1888), p. 34. Thus Horne also discussed "The Illustrations to the Quadriregio," a poem by Federico Frezzi, Bishop of Foligno in the early fifteenth century, which was published first in 1481.

28. In the John Rylands Library, Manchester.

29. Lyall Aubryson [pseud. of Horne], "The Letters and Papers of Adam Legendre: Now First Published from a Manuscript in the Possession of the Editor," *Century Guild Hobby Horse*, 6 (1891), pp. 56-57.

30. Ibid., p. 59.

31. The decoration was never concluded. Helen Combe completed the tempera decoration on the inside of the lid; Image, the lettering; while Horne executed the design about the keyboard; but the outside remained unfinished, though was temporarily coated in green lacquer so as to be ready for the exhibition of 1896.

CHAPTER 6   The Typographer and Book Design

1. *Fortnightly Review*, 56 (1894), p. 717. Horne at this time also contributed to the *Magazine of Art* and to the *Architectural Review*.

2. *The Binding of Books: An Essay in the History of Gold-Tooled Bindings* (London: Kegan Paul, Trench, Trüber & Co., 1894), p. 207.

3. Ibid., p. 208.

4. Ibid., pp. 212-13.

5. Robert Steele, *The Revival of Printing* (London: Macmillan, 1912).

6. *Studio*, 1, p. 26.

7. *Fortnightly Review*, 52 (1893), 319-25.

8. Ibid., 74

9. See Naum Gabo Pevsner, "The Architecture of Mannerism," *Mint*, 1 (1894), pp. 116-18.

10. *Wales England Wed: An Autobiography by Earnest Rhys* (London: J. M. Dent, 1940), pp. 152-53.

11. There is mention of an agreement between Mackmurdo and Horne dated 10 October 1894, in Bodley, MS Eng. Letters e 39.

12. Ibid.

13. From a typescript in my possession. The location of the original I do not know. Ironically later on Horne was complaining to Bernard Berenson that Jepson had left King's Bench Walk owing money for rent.

14. From a typescript in my possession.

15. *Morning Leader*, 1 August 1900, p. 4.

16. Ibid., 14 August 1900, p. 4.

17. See the Appendix for a list of some of Horne's periodical writings.

CHAPTER 7   The Art Historian: Italy and Botticelli

1. In the collection of Mrs. T. C. Dugdale.

2. Ibid.

3. Ibid.

4. In the possession of Mrs. N. Gray, Lawrence Binyon's daughter.

5. Ibid.

6. Ernest Rhys tells us that Horne sent him, as a wedding present, a print of Parmigianino. Writing on 9 February 1890, Horne describes it as "one of the most beautiful of the chiaroscuro prints; I am inclined to think it was cut by Antonio of Trent. . . . The triangular composition in the oval is very beautiful; as well as being in the most erudite taste of the Roman school." *Letters from Limbo* (London: J. M. Dent, 1936), p. 96.

7. William Rothenstein. *Men and Memories: Recollections of William Rothenstein* (London: Faber & Faber, 1931), p. 122.

8. *The Selected Letters of Bernard Berenson*, A. K. McComb, ed. (Boston: Houghton Mifflin, 1965), pp. 64-65.

9. *Robert Ross: Friend of Friends. Letters to Robert Ross*, Margery Ross, ed. (London: Cape, 1952), p. 144.

10. From the letters of Bernard and Mary Berenson and Mary Berenson's journal in the archives of Villa I Tatti, Settignano.

11. *Selected Letters of Bernard Berenson*, pp. 79-80.

12. Ibid. p. xi.

13. *Robert Ross: Friend of Friends,* p. 220. Horne had reviewed Max's Works in "The Precocious School of Humour," *Saturday Review,* 82 (1896), p. 221.

14. Not, however, according to J. Pope-Hennessy, *Uccello, Paolo di Dono* (London: Phaidon Press, 1950), p. 151, who describes the Louvre painting as the best preserved of the three. Horne's consistent polemic against the National Gallery and the purchases of its director, Sir Edward Poynter, is described in C. J. Holmes, *Self and Partners (mostly Self) Being the Reminiscences of C. J. Holmes* (London: Constable, 1936), p. 190.

15. See also "The Story of a Famous Botticelli," *Monthly Review* (1902).

16. See *Academy,* No. 1135, pp. 109-110.

17. Ibid., p. 110.

18. *Academy,* No. 1136, p. 133.

19. Anderson's comments from *Academy,* No. 1140, p. 214.

20. Letters from Horne to Warburg are to be found in the archive of the Warburg Institute, London. Those from Warburg to Horne in the collection of Mrs. T. C. Dugdale.

21. *Robert Ross: Friend of Friends,* p. 145.

22. This and following quotations from Horne's *Alessandro Filipepi, commonly called Sandro Botticelli, painter of Florence* (London: Bell & Sons, 1908). Only 240 copies were printed, of which 225 were for sale. Rpt. as *Botticelli: Painter of Florence,* John Pope-Hennessy, intro. (Princeton: Princeton University Press, 1980).

23. Comments by Lionello Venturi are from his *The History of Art Criticism,* Charles Marriott, trans. (New York: E. P. Dutton, 1936).

24. William Rothenstein, *Men and Memories 1872-1900* (London: 1931), p. 240.

25. Roger Fry, "Mr. Horne's Book on Botticelli," *Burlington Magazine,* 13 (1908), pp. 83-87.

26. See *The Art of Victorian Prose,* George Lewis Levine and William Madden, eds. (New York: Oxford University Press, 1968), pp. 39-52.

CHAPTER 8   The Final Phase

1. Quotations from *Samson Unshorn* are taken from Stanley Weintraub's *Reggie: A Portrait of Reginald Turner* (New York: G. Braziller, 1965), pp. 137-38. Professor Weintraub views Fawn as primarily an image of Duveen and only secondarily of Horne. I agree that it is a composite, but believe that there is more of Horne and Duveen.

2. See *Max Beerbohm's Letters to Reggie Turner,* Rupert Hart-Davis, ed. (London: Rupert Hart-Davis, 1964), pp. 191

3. Ibid., 245.

4. Horne was still at his old address in Florence, 8 Lung'arno degli Archibusiere in November 1912.

5. MS Houghton Library, Harvard University.

6. Letter in Mrs. T. C. Dugdale's collection.

7. *Lacerba*, 2, No. 7 (April 1914). "Il Massacro delle Donne" is to be found on pp. 97-99.

8. *Illustrated Catalogue of the Horne Museum*, Florence, 1926, pp. 8-10.

9. Ibid.

10. Weintraub, *Reggie: A Portrait of Reginald Turner.*

11. From the collection of Mrs. T. C. Dugdale.

12. Mary Berenson, however, in a letter to her husband on 16 April 1909 reports that "Horne said he had given up all idea of writing the second volume, on Botticelli's school." Lee Warner's letter is in the collection of Mrs. T. C. Dugdale.

13. From the collection of Mrs. T. C. Dugdale.

14. Ibid.

15. Ibid.

16. Ibid.

17. Fritz Saxl, *Lectures* (London: Warburg Institute, University of London, 1957), p. 335.

18. *Letters from Limbo* (London: J. M. Dent, 1936), p. 97.

Appendix

Horne's Holograph List:
Notebook at the Museo Horne

Some items on this list can definitely identified as Mackmurdo's design: for example, the chair with fretted back (presumably identical with the pair now in the William Morris Gallery, Walthamstow). However, some items are undoubtedly original designs by Horne himself.

The Ecclesiastical chintz is almost certainly the design of haloed trumpeters also in the William Morris Gallery. The figures are set in a background of swirling stems recalling the briars of Image's design for the cover of the *Century Guild Hobby Horse*.

A similar swirling movement, representing moonlight against which naked vague figures swim, is encountered in the illustration Horne furnished for the poem "Love I cannot hold thee longer" in the *Century Guild Hobby Horse* (1884).

Swirls and stylized leaning flowers, recalling Mackmurdo's design for the title-page of his *Wren's City Churches* (1883), appear in Horne's woodcut "Black Hail will Burst," now among the Horne designs at the Victoria and Albert Museum. Horne shows, therefore, the proto-art nouveau idiom of his colleagues, Mackmurdo and Image, though he later vehemently repudiated that style.

His pencil drawing of the huntress goddess, *Silvarum Potens: Diana Candida*, has the rectangular form typical of the *Century Guild's* later essays in book design and can be compared and contrasted with some of Beardsley's stiffly androgynous images in the *Later Work*.

Horne's initials for the *Century Guild Hobby Horse* with the letters forming part of a stylized floral design are related to Image's lettering among stylized flowers for the cover of "Michael Field's" *Stephania* (1892) and Ernest Radford's *Poems New and Old* (1895). Image is also a presence in Horne's borders and tail-pieces.

• Indicates works sold

Design for small cretonne
• Design for cretonne butterfly background
Design for tapestry. Lines and ivy leaves
Design for chair. Hawkes

• Design for chair. Fretted back
Design for tall Library Chair. Plain
• Design for casket. Image paintings
• Design for fender. (Doyley Carte)
• Design for Glass 3 panels and felt below
Design ditto altered without fret
Design Ecclesiastical chintz (Praise of the Soul)
Design Acanthus leaf chintz small
Design for stamped leather chair seat
Design 4 panels for Mackmurdo's Cabinet (Berberry)
Design 3 panels cartoon set in oils (Be ways of beauty)
Design ditto conventional tree. Both for glass
Design for cabinet (C. Vigers)

Drawings

Design'd picture. Black Hail will burst
Design'd picture. Then that day did etc.
Oil. The tree of praise
Water colour. "Come soon, soon."
Water colour. Landscape with a horse. (sketch)
Water colour. Landscape over the weald (sketch)
Water colour. Landscape done at the same time (sketch)
Water colour. Design. I heard an angel. (Brightwell) (sketch)
Chalk head. The torrid and the frigid interwove
Landscape sketch. Image
The four poplar. (Design water colour)
Pencil Drawing of Hobby Horse   F.P.
First sketch and lithograph
The Reredos Whissendine Church

Miscellaneous

Wood Black for Black Hail
2 Wood Black   after Image
Wood Black   small landscape CGH.H
7 Chairs painting
Cabinet painting (Mackmurdo)
Set of designs (all adored etc.) Image
Designs and 5 copper plate: 7 stray cats

Collections of Manuscripts

Bodelian. Oxford. MS Eng. Misc. 188
Bodelian. Oxford. MS Eng Letters. e. 38, e. 39
British Library, London. Add. MS 46363
Dolmetsch Museum, Haslemere
Mrs. T. C. Dugdale, London
Fonds Doucet. Bibliothèque Saint Geneviève, Paris
Mrs. N. Gray, Oxford
Museo Horne, Florence
Houghton Library, Harvard, Massachusetts
Professor A. W. Patrick, Hamilton, Ontario
John Rylands Library, Manchester
Villa I Tatti, Settignano
Victoria and Albert Museum, London, E 1136, 1147, 1151-1920
Warburg Institute, London
William Morris Gallery, Walthamstow. Century Guild MSS

Books by Herbert Horne
Arranged Chronologically

Hesperides: Poems by Robert Herrick. Edited with notes. Introduction by Ernest
  Rhys. London: W. Scott, 1887.
Diversi Colores. London: Chiswick Press, 1891. Rpt. Portland, ME: Bibleot,
  1908.
The Binding of Books. An Essay in the History of Gold-Tooled Bindings.
  London: Kegan Paul, Trench, Trüber, 1894.
*The Life of Leonardo di Vinci by Giorgio Vasari, done into English from the
  text of the second edition of the 'Lives'.* Commentary by Herbert Horne.
  London: Morrison and Gibb, 1903.
*The Life of Michelagnola Bvonarroti, Collected by Ascanio Condivi da la Ripa
  Transone.* Boston: D. B. Updike, 1904.
Nero and Other Plays. Edited with introduction and notes. London: T. Fisher
  Unwin, 1904.
Alessandro Filipepi, Commonly called Sandro Botticelli, Painter, of Florence.
  G. Bell & Sons, 1908. Rpt. as *Botticelli: Painter of Florence,* John Pope-
  Hennessy, intro. Princeton: Princeton University Press, 1980.
The Thoughts of the Emperor Marcus Aurelius Antoninus. Portland, ME:
  Bibelot, 1912.

Articles by Herbert Horne

The Century Guild Hobby Horse

"Nescio quae mugarum: No. 1. At the Charterhouse," 1 (1886), 77.

"A Study of Inigo Jones," 1 (1886), 123.

"The Life Mask of William Blake," 2 (1887), 29.

"Nescio quae mugarum: No. IV. Carols from the Coal-Fields," 2 (1887), 76.

"Nescio quae mugarum: No. VI. St. Mary-le-Strand," 2 (1887), 160.

"Note Upon Blake's Sibylline Leaf on Homer and Virgil," 2 (1887), 115.

"Potentia Silentii: Being a Selection of Passages from the Letters and Papers of James Smethan," 2 (1887), 123.

"Thoughts towards a Criticism of the Works of Dante Gabriel Rossetti," 2 (1887), 91.

"A Brief Note Upon *The Winter's Tale*," 3 (1888), 109.

"Potentia Silentii: Being a Further Selection of Passages from the Letters and Papers of James Smethan," 3 (1888), 8.

"New Reredos at Saint Paul's, Considered in Relation to the Whole Design of that Cathedral," 3 (1888), 72.

"Notes on the 'Quadriregio' of Federico Frezzi, by Richard Garnett, to Which are Prefixed Some Remarks upon the Principles of Wood-Cutting," 3 (1888), 34.

[Lyall Aubryson.] "The Letters and Papers of Adam Legendre: Now First Published from a Manuscript, in the Possession of the Editor," 5 (1890), 91.

"Notes upon Luca Cambiso's Woodcut of Aphrodite," 5 (1890), 161.

"Notes upon the Lyrical Ballads of Wordsworth," 5 (1890), 170.

"A Preface," 4 (1889), 1.

"Some Account of the Life and Public Works of James Gibbs, Architect," 4 (1889), 29.

"Some Account of the Life and Public Works of James Gibbs, Architect (Continued)," 4 (1889), 71.

"Some Account of the Life and Public Works of James Gibbs, Architect (Concluded)," 4 (1889), 110.

"A Brief Notice of Edward Calvert, Painter and Engraver," 6 (1891), 113.

[Lyall Aubryson.] "The Letters and Papers of Adam Legendre: Now First Published from a Manuscript in the Possession of the Editor (Continued)," 6 (1891), 45.

"A Note Upon the Picture of *A Roman Lady in the Decadence of the Empire* by G. F. Watts, R.A.," 6 (1891), 39.

"Some Considerations of the Nature of Fine Art: Being a Paper Read Before the Students of the Whitechapel Craft School, in Little Alie Street, on 26th of April, MDCCCXCI," 6 (1891), 83.

"William Bell Scott, Poet. Painter and Critic: Born 12 September, 1811; Died 22
   November, 1890," 6 (1891), 16.

The Hobby Horse

"An Essay in the Life of Inigo Jones: Architect, Cap. I.," Ns 1 (1893), 22.
"An Essay in the Life of Inigo Jones: Architect, Cap. II.," Ns 2 (1893), 64.
"The Ventures of Sir Balthazar Gerbier, Knight, Sometime Master of the
   Ceremonies to King Charles the First; Cap. I.," Ns 3 (1894), 97.

Articles on Renaissance Art History by Horne

"The Battle-Piece by Paolo Ucello, in the National Gallery," *Monthly Review*,
   5 (1901).
"Quelques Souvenirs de Sandro Botticelli," *Monthly Review*, 6 (1902).
"Some Leonardesque Questions," *Architectural Review*, 11 (1902).
"A Lost *Adoration of the Magi* by Sandro Botticelli," *Burlington Magazine*,
   1 (1903).
"Andrea del Castagno," *Burlington Magazine*, 7 (1904).
"A Newly Discovered Altar Piece by Alesso Baldovinetti," *Burlington
   Magazine*, 8 (1905).
"A Newly Discovered *Libro di Ricordi* of Alesso Baldovinetti," *Burlington
   Magazine*, 8 (1905-1906).
"Il Graffione," *Burlington Magazine*, 8 (1905-1906).
"Giovanni dal Ponte," *Burlington Magazine*, 9 (1906).
"Jacopo del Sellaio," *Burlington Magazine*, 13 (1908).
"A Lost *Adoration of the Magi*," *Burlington Magazine*, 16 (1909-1910).
"La Tavola D'Altare delle Convertite Dipinta da Sandro Botticelli," *Rassagna
   D'Arte*, September 1913.
"Notes on Luca della Robia," *Burlington Magazine*, 28 (1915-1916).
"The Last Communion of Saint Jerome of Sandro Botticelli," *Bulletin of the
   Metropolitan Museum of Art*, 28 (1915). This was reprinted in abridged
   form in *Burlington Magazine*, 28 (1915-1916).

Miscellaneous

"Indigo Jones," in *The Dictionary of National Biography* (1892).
Introduction to Randall Davies's, *Chelsea Old Church* (1904).

Unsigned Articles by Horne

Cuttings of Horne's generally unsigned journalism survive in the archives of the Museo Horne, Florence. Each is marked "H.P.H." in his own hand. There are, on occasion, corrections and additional material. Horne also preserved some of Symons's reviews. Some of the following were signed with "H". The list is probably not exhaustive.

Saturday Review

1894

"Colour in Architecture."	10	November
"The New English Art Club."	24	November
"Pen Drawing."	24	November
"Houses and Furniture."	1	December
"The Fine Arts in Technical Schools."	8	December
"The Sforza Book of Hours, Supplement."	10	December
"Bach and the Harpsichord."	15	December
"Rembrandt van Ryn."	22	December

1895

"The Exhibition of Venetian Art."	5	January
"A History of Painting."	5	January
"The Fairest Church in all the World."	12	January
"The Wood Beyond the World."	26	January
"Nollekens."	23	March
"Book Plates."	23	March
"Peterborough Cathedral."	6	April
"The Royal Society of Painters in Watercolour."	27	April
"The Salon and the Royal Academy."	11	May
"The Champ de Mars."	18	May
"Architecture at the Academy."	25	May
"Le Gallienne, The Poetaster."	25	May
"The Poet as Theologian."	8	June

1896

"A Review of Pater's *Miscellaneous Studies.*"	1	August
"The Arts and Crafts at the New Gallery."	3	October

| "The History of Architecture." | 24 | October |
| "William Morris as Printer." | 24 | December |

1897

"Albert Moore."	16	January
"Byzantine Architecture in Italy."	17	April
"Decorative Art in England, Supplement."	12	June
"Thomas Hope Maclachlan."	12	June
"The National Gallery."	12	June
"Jubilee Decorations."	26	June
"Madox Brown."	10	July
"Italian Renaissance Architecture."	17	July
"Memorials of Christies."	31	July
"A Life of Constable."	21	August
"The Best Scenery that I Knew."	28	August

"In brief, excepting the human form,
    I take architecture to be the better
    part of scenery." The President of
    the Royal Academy 28th August on art critics.
    The Tate Gallery.   23   October

1898

"The State of the National		
Gallery, Supplement."	26	February
Ghirlandaio's Fresco Portrait of		
Arrigo Vespucci."	4	March
"Botticelli and Savonarola."	13	August

1900

"The Waddesdon Bequest."	14	April
"Illuminated Manuscripts."	21	September
"A Careless Handbook to the		
Florentine Painters."	12	October
"Illuminated Manuscripts."	2	July

The Review of the Week

1899

| "*Bernardo Luini* by G. C. Williamson." | 30 | December |

1900

"*Andrea del Sarto* by H. Guinness."	6	January
"The Van Dyke Exhibition."	6	January
"The Van Dyke Exhibition. (Second Notice)."	13	January
"*Pompeii, Its Life and Art* by August Mav."	20	January
"The Genius of Ruskin."	27	January

Horne has a note: "The gist of the first paragraph,
and some other points in this article, I had from
Selwyn Image, who studied under Ruskin at Oxford."

"Our National Gallery."	27	January

Horne inserts a correction: "No. 592
and No. 1033 have been attributed to
Botticelli. Now Morelli."

"The Tomb of Saint Peter."	3	February
"August Rodin."	10	February
"A Newly Discovered Botticelli."	17	February
"A Disagreeable Genius."	16	June

The Londonder

1900

"Correggio."	21	April
"The Pictures at the Royal Academy I."	12	May
"The Pictures at the Royal Academy II."	19	May
"Architecture at the Royal Academy."	2	June
"Sculpture at the Royal Academy."	16	June
"The Wallace Collection."	30	June
"Thomas Girtin."	4	August

The Morning Leader

1900

"The Fine Arts" [On Mrs Stanhope Forbes at the Fine Arts Society; Mrs John Tweed private view and others].	3	April
"Art Notes" [On The Society of British Artists; the New English Art Club and Charles Conder at Messrs. Carfax].	10	April

"Art Notes" [On Baron Rothschild Bequest
    at the British Museum; the Barbizon school
    and others at Messrs. McLean; and other
    London exhibitions].   17   April
"Art Notes" [On Watts, Sargent, Whistler
    and others].   25   April
"Art Notes" [On Watts and others at the
    New Gallery; Walter Crane and others
    at the Old Water Colour Society].   2   May
"The Royal Academy. First Notice" [On Watts,
    Orchardson and others].   5   May
"Art Notes" [On Monticelli at the Goupil Gallery;
    Sir John Tenniel, R. Ponsonby Staples and
    others at the Fine Art Society; A. E. Enslie
    at Old Water Colour Society].   15   May
"The Royal Academy. Second Notice"
    [On Frank Dicksee, La Thangue and others].   23   May

"Art Notes" [On C. H. Shannon at the Dutch Gallery;
    and on several other London exhibitions].   29   May
"Art Notes" [On the Dudley Gallery Art Society;
    early Italian, Flemish and Dutch schools at
    the Dowdeswell Gallery; and on several other
    London exhibitions].   13   June
"Art Notes" [On Rembrandt and his school at the
    Burlington Fine Arts].   19   June
"The Wallace Collection. First Notice" [On Titian's
    Perseus and Andromeda among others].   26   June

1901

"Art Notes" [On Watts, Sargent and others in
    the Summer Exhibition at the New Gallery].   29   April
"The Royal Academy. First Notice" [On Watts,
    Sargent, Benjamin Constant, George Clausen
    and others].   6   May
"The Royal Academy. Second Notice" [On J. J. Shannon,
    Sargent, Hubert von Herkomer and others].   22   May
"Drawings at the British Museum" [On drawings by
    Michelangelo, Rembrandt, Watteau, Hogarth and
    others included in the Henry Vaughan Bequest]. 27   May
"Art Notes" [On drawings by Hogarth, Cozens and others
    included among the English drawings at the
    British Museum].   8   June

"Art Notes" [On Conder, Corot, Fantin-Latour
    and others].   21   June
"Art Notes" [On Miss Fortescue-Brickdale,
    Byam Shaw and the "New Pre-Raphaelites"].   28   June
"Art Notes" [On Clausen, Muhrmann, Rodin and others
    at the Pastel Society exhibition].   5   July
"Art Notes" [On Mariano Fortuny].   19   July
"Art Notes" [On the finances of the Royal Academy].   2   August
"Art Notes" [Previous article continued.
    On the National Portrait Gallery].   9   August
"Art Notes" [On the Spanish Exhibition, in particular
    Velasquez at the Guildhall].   19   August
"Art Notes" [Previous article continued.
    On Velasques, El Greco, Goya].   30   August

1902

"Art Notes" [On C. H. Shannon at the Dutch Gallery].   20   June
"Art Notes" [On Steer and early Italian pictures
    at Messrs. Carfax].   1   July
"Art Notes" [On Tuke, Clausen, Muhrmann and others
    at the exhibition of the Pastel Society].   11   July
"Art Notes" [On Byam Shaw at Dowdeswell's; and
    Miss William's private exhibition].   30   July

1904

"The Royal Academy. Mr. Watts and Physical Energy
    in Bronze. First Notice" [On sculpture by Watts,
    Sargent and others].   2   May
"The English Titian. Notes and Memories of
    Mr. G. F. Watts" [Obituary essay].   2   July
"Art Notes. The Heritage of a Failure"
    [On John Sell Cotman].   25   August

Dissertations

Block, Lilian. "*The Pursuit of Beauty*: The Background and Creators of the
    Hobby Horse Magazine." M.A. Dissertation, Columbia University (1965).
Campbell, Louisa. "Herbert Horne and the Arts and Crafts Movement."
    Unpublished B.A. Dissertation. Sussex, 1973.
Fletcher, Ian. "Union and Beauty: An Examination of Some Nineteenth
    Century Minority Periodicals." Ph.D. Reading, 1965. 2 vols.

Haslam, W. M. P. "The Theory and Designs of A. H. Mackmurdo." M.A. Courtauld Institute, 1968.

Hunt, Loraine Rose Lively. "*The Century Guild Hobby Horse*: A Study of a Magazine." Ph.D. Dissertation, University of North Carolina (1965).

Tickner, S. E. "Selwyn Image: His Life, Work and Associations." Ph.D. Reading, 1970. 2 vols.

Books About and Relating to Horne

Catalogue of A. H. Mackmurdo and The Guild Collection. William Morris Gallery, Walthamstow.

Collobi, L. R. *Disegni inglesi della Fondazione Horne in Firenze.* Milano, 1966.

Davies, Randall. "Introduction" in *The Burlington Fine Art Club Collection of Mr. Herbert Horne's Collection of Drawings*, 1916.

Harper, G. *English Pen Artists of Today. Examples of their work, some criticisms and appreciations.* 1892.

Illustrated Catalogue of the Horne Museum. Florence, 1926. The introduction is by Conte Gamba and was first published in 1921 in Italian.

Saxl, Fritz. *Lectures.* London: Warburg Institute, University of London, 1957.

Steele, Robert. *The Revival of Printing.* London: Macmillan, 1912.

Sutton, Denys *The Letters of Roger Fry.* New York: Random House, 1972. I.

Articles About and Relating to Horne

Anthony, E. W. "The Horne House, Florence," *House Beautiful*, November 1922.

Berenson, Mary. "Obituary," *Rassegna D'Arte*, 16 (1916).

Brockwell, N. W. "The Herbert Horne Foundation, Florence (Fondazione Herbert Horne)," *Nineteenth Century*, May 1922.

Fry, Roger. "Mr. Horne's Book on Botticelli," *Burlington Magazine*, 13 (1908), 83-87.

———. "Obituary," *The Burlington Magazine*, 29 (1916).

Gamba, Conte. "Il Palazzo della Raccolto Horne a Firenze," *Dedalo*, 1 (1925).

Harbron, D. "Minor Masters of the Nineteenth Century. Notes on Some Lesser Known Architects, VII. Herbert Horne: The Critic as Artist," *Architectural Review*, 81 (January-June 1937).

Rusconi, A. J. "The Horne Collection in Florence," *Connoisseur*, 63 (May 1922).

Symons, Arthur. "The Hobby Horse," *Vanity Fair*, 18 (1922).

———. "Unpublished Letters of Verlaine," *North American Review*, 201, 202 (1915).

Turner, R. "Herbert Horne," *Anglo-Italian Review*, October 1918.

Vallance, A. "Mr. Arthur M. Mackmurdo and the Century Guild," *Studio*, 16 (1899).

General Works of Interest on Horne

The Academy, Nos. 1135, 1136, 1140 (February, March 1894).

Berenson, Richard. *Selected Letters*. A. K. McComb, ed. Boston: Houghton, Mifflin, 1964.

Beerbohm, Max. *Letters to Reggie Turner*. Rupert Hart-Davis, ed. New York: Rupert Hart-Davis, 1965.

————. *A Catalogue of the Caricatures*. Rupert Hart-Davis, comp. Cambridge: Harvard University Press, 1972.

Campbell, Margaret. *Dolmetsch: The Man and his Work*. Seattle: University of Washington Press, 1975.

Charles Ricketts and Charles Shannon: An Aesthetic Partnership. Catalogue by Stephen Calloway and Paul Delaney. London: Borough of Richmond on Thorner, 1979.

Dolmetsch, Mabel. *Personal Recollections of Arnold Dolmetsch*. London: Routledge, 1958.

Dearmer, Nancy, ed. *The Life of Percy Dearmer*. London: Jonathan Cape, 1940.

Dowson, Ernest. *The Letters of Ernest Dowson*, Desmond Flower and Henry Maas, eds. London: Cassell, 1967.

Ettlinger, Leopold D. *Botticelli*. London: Thames and Hudson, 1976.

Fletcher, Ian. "Bedford Park: Aesthete's Elysium?" *Romantic Mythologies*. London: Routledge & Kegan Paul, 1967.

Hassall, Christopher. *Edward Marsh: Patron of the Arts*. London: Longmans, 1959.

Holmes, C. J. *Self and Partners (mostly Self) Being the Reminiscences of C. J. Holmes*. London: Constable, 1936.

Jepson, Edgar. *Memoirs of a Victorian*. London: Victor Gollancz 1933.

Lago, Mary and Karl Beckson, eds. *Max and Will: Max Beerbohm and William Rothenstein: Their friendship and letters 1893 to 1945*. Cambridge: Harvard University Press, 1975.

Plarr, Victor. *Ernest Dowson, 1888-1897 Reminiscences, Unpublished Letters and Marginalia*. London: Elkin Mathews, 1914.

Rhys, Ernest. *Everyman Remembers*. London: J. M. Dent, 1931.

————. *Letters from Limbo*. London: J. M. Dent, 1936.

————. *Wales England Wed: An Autobiography by Earnest Rhys*. London: J. M. Dent, 1940.

Ross, Margery, ed. *Robert Ross: Friend of Friends. Letters to Robert Ross, Art Critic and Writer, Together with Extracts from His Published Articles.* London: Cape, 1952.

Rothenstein, Sir William. *Men and Memories: Recollections of William Rothenstein, 1872-1900.* London: Faber & Faber, 1931.

————. *Men and Memories, 1900-1922.* London: Faber & Faber, 1932.

Shields, Frederic. *The Life and Letters of Frederic Shields.* Ernestine Mills, ed. London: Longmans, Green, 1912.

Taylor, John Russell. *The Art Nouveau Book in Britain.* Edinburgh: P. Harris, 1980.

Thompson, Susan Otis. *American Book Design and William Morris.* New York: R. R. Bowker, 1977.

Underwood, Victor Philip. *Verlaine et l'Angleterre.* Paris: Librairie Nizet, 1956.

Weintraub, Stanley. *Reggie: A Portrait of Reginald Turner.* New York: G. Braziller, 1965.

Works and Days, from the Journal of Michael Field, T. & D.C. Sturge Moore, eds. London: John Murray, 1933.

Index

1880-1920 British Authors Series

Rediscovering Herbert Horne:
Poet, Architect, Typographer, Art Historian

Title-page, Contents page, Text

Designed by
Robert Langenfeld

Using WordPerfect 5.0
Typeface ITC Garamond

Dust Jacket

Designed by
Sheila P. Donohue
&
Sarah Nawrocki

Typeface Garamond

Printer: Thomson-Shore, Inc.
Production Coordinator, Diane Nourse
Dexter, Michigan U. S. A.
1990